At Issue

DISCARD

I Solar Storms

W9-AKB-799

Other Books in the At Issue Series:

Animal Experimentation

Are Abortion Rights Threatened?

Are Teen Boot Camps Effective?

Are Unions Still Relevant?

Child Pornography

The Children of Undocumented Immigrants

Club Drugs

Digitized Textbooks

Do Cell Phones Cause Cancer?

Embryonic and Adult Stem Cells

Fast Food

High School Dropouts

How Far Should Science Extend the Human Lifespan?

Is China's Economic Growth a Threat to America?

Reality TV

Road Rage

Should Drilling Be Permitted in the Arctic National Wildlife Refuge?

Should the Federal Income Tax Be Eliminated?

Teen Suicide

What Is the Future of the Music Industry?

What Is the Impact of Twitter?

At Issue

⎮ Solar Storms

Tamara Thompson, Book Editor

GREENHAVEN PRESS
A part of Gale, Cengage Learning

Detroit • New York • San Francisco • New Haven, Conn • Waterville, Maine • London

GALE
CENGAGE Learning·

Elizabeth Des Chenes, *Managing Editor*

© 2013 Greenhaven Press, a part of Gale, Cengage Learning.

Gale and Greenhaven Press are registered trademarks used herein under license.

For more information, contact:
Greenhaven Press
27500 Drake Rd.
Farmington Hills, MI 48331-3535
Or you can visit our Internet site at gale.cengage.com

For product information and technology assistance, contact us at

Gale Customer Support, 1-800-877-4253
For permission to use material from this text or product, submit all requests online at www.cengage.com/permissions.

Further permissions questions can be e-mailed to permissionrequest@cengage.com.

Articles in Greenhaven Press anthologies are often edited for length to meet page requirements. In addition, original titles of these works are changed to clearly present the main thesis and to explicitly indicate the author's opinion. Every effort is made to ensure that Greenhaven Press accurately reflects the original intent of the authors. Every effort has been made to trace the owners of copyrighted material.

Cover photograph © Sue Poynton. Image from BigStockPhoto.com.

LIBRARY OF CONGRESS CATALOGING-IN-PUBLICATION DATA

Solar storms / Tamara Thompson, book editor.
   p. cm. -- (At issue)
  Includes bibliographical references and index.
  ISBN 978-0-7377-6205-1 (hardcover) -- ISBN 978-0-7377-6206-8 (pbk.)
  1. Solar activity. 2. Solar activity--Forecasting. 3. Space environment. I. Thompson, Tamara.
  QB524.S58274 2012
  523.7'5--dc23

                   2012011593

Printed in the United States of America
1 2 3 4 5   16 15 14 13 12

FD254

Contents

Introduction   7

1. A Big Solar Storm Would Wreak   10
Global Socioeconomic Havoc
*National Research Council Committee on
the Societal and Economic Impacts of Severe
Space Weather Events*

2. Fears of Damage from Solar Storms   21
Are Overblown
Ian O'Neill

3. A Solar Storm Could Cripple Communications   30
and Power Grids Worldwide
Richard A. Lovett

4. The Current Solar Storm Cycle Will Be   35
Milder than Thought
*National Oceanic and Atmospheric
Administration (NOAA)*

5. Solar Storm Predictions Needlessly Inflame   39
2012 Doomsday Fears
Alan Boyle

6. Global Recovery from a Solar Storm   43
Could Take Years
Michael Brooks

7. Bracing the Satellite Infrastructure   53
for a Solar Superstorm
Sten F. Odenwald and James L. Green

8. The World Needs a Global Warning System   65
for Solar Storms
Dan Reynolds

9. NASA Hopes New "Solar Shield" Will   69
Predict Storm Severity
Nola Redd

10. Solar Storms Make Airplane Travel   74
    More Dangerous
    Patrick Lynch

11. Solar Storms Do Not Cause Global Warming   78
    Brian Handwerk

Organizations to Contact   83
Bibliography   89
Index   96

Introduction

On January 22, 2012, the sun let loose a big burst of energy—a massive explosion called a solar flare that hurtled charged particles and some of the sun's radioactive plasma toward Earth at the incredible speed of 621 miles per second. When that powerful electromagnetic burst, called a coronal mass ejection (CME), collided with the Earth's magnetic field, it produced the strongest solar storm the planet had seen in nearly a decade.

Broadcast media and the Internet were in a frenzy over dramatic satellite photos and awe-inspiring video of the volatile activity on the sun's surface. Major airlines were forced to reroute flights away from the Earth's poles to avoid communication disturbances and dangerous radiation. The normal displays of Earth's auroras, known as the northern and southern lights, were stunningly amplified. There were some dropped cell phone calls and scattered GPS problems.

But, all in all, the effect on the ground was minimal, considering the amplitude of the storm. That's because the CME hit the Earth's magnetic field at an angle, not directly. Simply put, it was just a glancing blow.

"Earth's magnetic field served as a shield, and pretty much shielded the radiation so that it doesn't penetrate that deep," Yihua Zheng, a lead researcher at the National Aeronautics and Space Administration (NASA) Goddard Space Flight Center, told the popular astronomy website Space.com shortly after the event. "It's like a car collision: head-on or off to the side. A CME is like that too. For this one, if it was a direct hit, Earth would receive a much stronger impact. This one was on an angle—toward higher latitudes and a little off the ecliptic—otherwise it would be a much stronger impact."

That's exactly what scientists fear could happen as the sun moves through its current 11-year cycle of waxing and waning, called Solar Cycle 24, which will reach its high point of activity—its solar maximum—in 2013. Experts warn that the powerful January 2012 storm could be a sign that the sun is becoming more active again after a long period of being relatively dormant. The January 2012 solar flare was designated an M9-class eruption, falling just short of being an X-class flare, the most powerful kind of solar storm. M-class flares are powerful but moderate, while C-class storms are weaker.

When the biggest solar storm on record, known as the Carrington Event, happened in 1859, a CME from an X-class flare caused a geomagnetic disturbance so powerful that it sent sparks shooting from telegraph machines, frying the main communications equipment of the day. If such a solar "superstorm" were to happen today, scientists predict, it could be utterly disastrous.

Experts agree that a direct CME hit from an X-class flare would cause a geomagnetic storm that could zap power grids across the globe and grind the world's modern technological infrastructure to a halt. It could take months or years to repair, and the socioeconomic impacts—both in the short- and long-term—could be devastating.

But why are solar storms suddenly such a big threat when they have been occurring since the beginning of the Solar System and the Earth has endured them without much difficulty up until now? Quite simply, it is because the world has never before been so dependent on vulnerable technologies like satellite telecommunications, cell phones, global positioning systems, tablet computers, and electricity-based systems such as the Internet for global commerce, security, health care, and communications.

"Many things we take for granted today are so much more prone to the effects of space weather than was the case during the last [solar] maximum," from 2000 to 2002, Jane Lubchenco, administrator for the National Oceanic and Atmospheric Administration, told the annual meeting of the American Association for the Advancement of Science in 2011. She added that the potential for a solar flare to disrupt the high-tech infrastructure means that it's time to get serious about the issue and raise public awareness. "We have every reason to expect we're going to be seeing more space weather in the coming years, and it behooves us to be smart and be prepared," she said.

While the science of predicting solar storms is still in its infancy, scientists at NASA and elsewhere are racing to improve their forecasting ability, equip more satellites with radiation shielding, and fortify power grids with resilient transformers and capacitors to minimize the damage when the time comes—as it eventually will. "As we enter into a period of enhanced solar activity, it seems pretty clear that we are going to be looking at the possibility of not only more solar events but also the possibility of some very strong events," Lubchenco said. "This is not a matter of if—it's simply a matter of when and how big."

The authors in *At Issue: Solar Storms* discuss the mechanics of solar storms and present a wide range of viewpoints on key topics, including solar storm prediction, the effect of space weather on human behavior and global warming, current infrastructure weaknesses, efforts to prepare, and likely scenarios for Solar Cycle 24 and its potential aftermath.

1

A Big Solar Storm Would Wreak Global Socioeconomic Havoc

National Research Council Committee on the Societal and Economic Impacts of Severe Space Weather Events

The Committee on the Societal and Economic Impacts of Severe Space Weather Events is a committee of the National Research Council, a nonprofit organization that conducts research for and provides expert advice to Congress and federal agencies.

Modern society depends heavily on technologies that are interdependent in a very complex way. For example, cell phones and Wi-fi signals depend on satellites, which in turn depend on global positioning systems, which in turn depend on electricity. If any or all of these elements are disrupted by a solar storm— especially the electrical power grid—the world would face severe socioeconomic consequences. Aside from the physical damage to the technologies themselves, the effects of a solar storm could include the global disruption of transportation, communication, banking, health care, and government services—even things like refrigeration of food and medicines and pumping of water and fuel, all of which depend on electricity. Experts estimate the economic cost of such a scenario to be in the trillions during the first year alone, and they say recovery could take years. More study of severe space weather and its possible impacts is urgently needed.

Modern society depends heavily on a variety of technologies that are susceptible to the extremes of space weather—severe disturbances of the upper atmosphere and of the near-Earth space environment that are driven by the magnetic activity of the Sun. Strong auroral currents can disrupt and damage modern electric power grids and may contribute to the corrosion of oil and gas pipelines. Magnetic storm-driven ionospheric density disturbances interfere with high-frequency (HF) radio communications and navigation signals from Global Positioning System (GPS) satellites, while polar cap absorption (PCA) events can degrade—and, during severe events, completely black out—HF communications along transpolar aviation routes, requiring aircraft flying these routes to be diverted to lower latitudes. Exposure of spacecraft to energetic particles during solar energetic particle events and radiation belt enhancements can cause temporary operational anomalies, damage critical electronics, degrade solar arrays, and blind optical systems such as imagers and star trackers.

The effects of space weather on modern technological systems are well documented in both the technical literature and popular accounts. Most often cited perhaps is the collapse within 90 seconds of northeastern Canada's Hydro-Quebec power grid during the great geomagnetic storm of March 1989, which left millions of people without electricity for up to 9 hours. This event exemplifies the dramatic impact that extreme space weather can have on a technology upon which modern society in all of its manifold and interconnected activities and functions critically depends.

Two Decades of Learning

Nearly two decades have passed since the March 1989 event. During that time, awareness of the risks of extreme space weather has increased among the affected industries, mitigation strategies have been developed, new sources of data have become available (e.g., the upstream solar wind measurements from the Advanced Composition Explorer), new models of the space environment have been created, and a national space weather infrastructure has evolved to provide data, alerts, and forecasts to an increasing number of users.

The main industries whose operations can be adversely affected by extreme space weather are the electric power, spacecraft, aviation, and GPS-based positioning industries.

Now, 20 years later and approaching a new interval of increased solar activity, how well equipped are we to manage the effects of space weather? Have recent technological developments made our critical technologies more or less vulnerable? How well do we understand the broader societal and economic impacts of extreme space weather events? Are our institutions prepared to cope with the effects of a "space weather Katrina," a rare, but according to the historical record, not inconceivable eventuality? On May 22 and 23, 2008, a workshop held in Washington, D.C., under the auspices of the National Research Council brought together representatives of industry, the federal government, and the social science community to explore these and related questions. This report was prepared by members of the ad hoc committee that organized the workshop, and it summarizes the key themes, ideas, and insights that emerged during the 1 ½ days of presentations and discussions.

The Impact of Space Weather

Modern technological society is characterized by a complex interweave of dependencies and interdependencies among its critical infrastructures. A complete picture of the socioeconomic impact of severe space weather must include both direct, industry-specific effects (such as power outages and spacecraft anomalies) and the collateral effects of space-weather-driven technology failures on dependent infrastructures and services.

The main industries whose operations can be adversely affected by extreme space weather are the electric power, spacecraft, aviation, and GPS-based positioning industries. The March 1989 blackout in Quebec and the forced outages of electric power equipment in the northeastern United States remain the classic example of the impact of a severe space weather event on the electric power industry. Several examples of the impact of space weather on the other industries are cited in the report:

- The outage in January 1994 of two Canadian telecommunications satellites during a period of enhanced energetic electron fluxes at geosynchronous orbit, disrupting communications services nationwide. The first satellite recovered in a few hours; recovery of the second satellite took 6 months and cost $50 million to $70 million.

- The diversion of 26 United Airlines flights to non-polar or less-than-optimum polar routes during several days of disturbed space weather in January 2005. The flights were diverted to avoid the risk of HF radio blackouts during PCA events. The increased flight time and extra landings and takeoffs required by such route changes increase fuel consumption and raise cost, while the delays disrupt connections to other flights.

- Disabling of the Federal Aviation Administration's recently implemented GPS-based Wide Area Augmentation System (WAAS) for 30 hours during the severe space weather events of October–November 2003.

Industries Work to Adapt

With increasing awareness and understanding of space weather effects on their technologies, industries have responded to the threat of extreme space weather through improved operational procedures and technologies. As just noted, airlines reroute flights scheduled for polar routes during intense solar energetic particle events in order to preserve reliable communications. Alerted to an impending geomagnetic storm by NOAA's Space Weather Prediction Center (SWPC) and monitoring ground currents in real-time, power grid operators take defensive measures to protect the grid against geomagnetically induced currents (GICs). Similarly, under adverse space weather conditions, launch personnel may delay a launch, and satellite operators may postpone certain operations (e.g., thruster firings). For the spacecraft industry, however, the primary approach to mitigating the effects of space weather is to design satellites to operate under extreme environmental conditions to the maximum extent possible within cost and resource constraints. GPS modernization, through the addition of two new navigation signals and new codes, is expected to help mitigate space weather effects (e.g., ranging errors, fading caused by ionospheric scintillation), although to what degree is not known. These technologies will come on line incrementally over the next 15 years as new GPS satellites become operational. In the meantime, the Federal Aviation Administration will maintain "legacy" non-GPS-based navigation systems as a backup, while other GPS users (e.g., offshore drilling companies) can postpone operations for which precision position knowledge is required until the ionospheric disturbance is over.

Socioeconomic Impacts

Because of the interconnectedness of critical infrastructures in modern society, the impacts of severe space weather events can go beyond disruption of existing technical systems and lead to short-term as well as to long-term collateral socioeconomic disruptions. Electric power is modern society's cornerstone technology, the technology on which virtually all other infrastructures and services depend. Although the probability of a wide-area electric power blackout resulting from an extreme space weather event is low, the consequences of such an event could be very high, as its effects would cascade through other, dependent systems. Collateral effects of a longer-term outage would likely include, for example, disruption of the transportation, communication, banking, and finance systems, and government services; the breakdown of the distribution of potable water owing to pump failure; and the loss of perishable foods and medications because of lack of refrigeration. The resulting loss of services for a significant period of time in even one region of the country could affect the entire nation and have international impacts as well.

The occurrence today of an event like the 1921 storm would result in large-scale blackouts affecting more than 130 million people.

Extreme space weather events are low-frequency/high-consequence (LF/HC) events and as such present—in terms of their potential broader, collateral impacts—a unique set of problems for public (and private) institutions and governance, different from the problems raised by conventional, expected, and frequently experienced events. As a consequence, dealing with the collateral impacts of LF/HC events requires different types of budgeting and management capabilities and consequently challenges the basis for conventional policies and risk management strategies, which assume a universe of constant or reliable conditions. Moreover, because systems can quickly become dependent on new technologies in ways that are unknown and unexpected to both developers and users, vulnerabilities in one part of the broader system have a tendency to spread to other parts of the system. Thus, it is difficult to understand, much less to predict, the consequences of future LF/HC events. Sustaining preparedness and planning for such events in future years is equally difficult.

Future Vulnerabilities

Our knowledge and understanding of the vulnerabilities of modern technological infrastructure to severe space weather and the measures developed to mitigate those vulnerabilities are based largely on experience and knowledge gained during the past 20 or 30 years, during such episodes of severe space weather as the geomagnetic superstorms of March 1989 and October–November 2003. As severe as some of these recent events have been, the historical record reveals that space weather of even greater severity has occurred in the past— e.g., the Carrington event of 1859 and the great geomagnetic storm of May 1921—and suggests that such extreme events, though rare, are likely to occur again some time in the future. While the socioeconomic impacts of a future Carrington event are difficult to predict, it is not unreasonable to assume that an event of such magnitude would lead to much deeper and more widespread socioeconomic disruptions than occurred in 1859, when modern electricity-based technology was still in its infancy.

A more quantitative estimate of the potential impact of an unusually large space weather event has been obtained by ex-amining the effects of a storm of the magnitude of the May 1921 superstorm on today's electric power infrastructure. De-spite the lessons learned since 1989 and their successful appli-cation during the October–November 2003 storms, the nation's electric power grids remain vulnerable to disruption and damage by severe space weather and have become even more so, in terms of both widespread blackouts and perma-nent equipment damage requiring long restoration times. Ac-cording to a study by the Metatech Corporation, the occur-rence today of an event like the 1921 storm would result in large-scale blackouts affecting more than 130 million people and would expose more than 350 transformers to the risk of permanent damage.

The Space Weather Infrastructure

Space weather services in the United States are provided primarily by NOAA's SWPC and the U.S. Air Force's (USAF's) Weather Agency (AFWA), which work closely together to address the needs of their civilian and military user communities, respectively. The SWPC draws on a variety of data sources, both space- and ground-based, to provide forecasts, watches, warnings, alerts, and summaries as well as operational space weather products to civilian and commercial users. Its primary sources of information about solar activity, upstream solar wind conditions, and the geospace environment are NASA's Advanced Composition Explorer (ACE), NOAA's GOES and POES satellites, magnetometers, and the USAF's solar observing networks. Secondary sources include SOHO and STEREO as well as a number of ground-based facilities. Despite a small and unstable budget (roughly $6 million to $7 million U.S. dollars annually) that limits capabilities, the SWPC has experienced a steady growth in customer base, even during the solar minimum years, when disturbance activity is lower. The focus of the USAF's space weather effort is on providing situational knowledge of the real-time space weather environment and assessments of the impacts of space weather on different Department of Defense missions. The Air Force uses NOAA data combined with data from its own assets such as the Defense Meteorological Satellites Program satellites, the Communications/Navigation Outage Forecasting System, the Solar Electro-Optical Network, the Digital Ionospheric Sounding System, and the GPS network.

> One of the important functions of a nation's space weather infrastructure is to provide reliable long-term forecasts.

NASA is the third major element in the nation's space weather infrastructure. Although NASA's role is scientific rather than operational, NASA science missions such as ACE provide critical space weather information, and NASA's Living with a Star program targets research and technologies that are relevant to operations. NASA-developed products that are candidates for eventual transfer from research to operations include sensor technology and physics-based space weather models that can be transitioned into operational tools for forecasting and situational awareness.

Other key elements of the nation's space weather infrastructure are the solar and space physics research community and the emerging commercial space weather businesses. Of particular importance are the efforts of these sectors in the area of model development.

Space Weather Forecasting: Capabilities and Limitations

One of the important functions of a nation's space weather infrastructure is to provide reliable long-term forecasts, although the importance of forecasts varies according to industry. With long-term (1- to 3-day) forecasts and minimal false alarms, the various user communities can take actions to mitigate the effects of impending solar disturbances and to minimize their economic impact. Currently, NOAA's SWPC can make probability forecasts of space weather events with varying degrees of success. For example, the SWPC can, with moderate confidence, predict the occurrence probability of a geomagnetic storm or an X-class flare 1 to 3 days in advance, whereas its capability to provide even short-term (less than 1 day) or long-term forecasts of ionospheric disturbances—information important for GPS users—is poor. The SWPC has identified a number of critical steps needed to improve its forecasting capability, enabling it, for example, to provide high-confidence long- and short-term forecasts of geomagnetic storms and ionospheric disturbances. These steps include securing an operational solar wind monitor at L1; transitioning research models (e.g., of coronal mass ejection propagation, the geospace radiation environment, and the coupled magnetosphere/ionosphere/atmosphere system) into operations, and developing precision GPS forecast and correction tools. The requirement for a solar wind monitor at L1 is particularly important because ACE, the SWPC's sole source of real-time upstream solar wind and interplanetary magnetic field data, is well beyond its planned operational life, and provisions to replace it have not been made.

The Report Is Only a Starting Point

The title of the workshop on which this report is based, "The Societal and Economic Impacts of Severe Space Weather Events," perhaps promised more than this subsequent report can fully deliver. What emerged from the presentations and discussions at the workshop is that the invited experts understand well the effects of at least moderately severe space weather on specific technologies, and in many cases know what is required to mitigate them, whether enhanced forecasting and monitoring capabilities, new technologies (new GPS signals and codes, new-generation radiation-hardened electronics), or improved operational procedures. Limited information was also provided—and captured in this report—on the costs of space weather-induced outages (e.g., $50 million to $70 million to restore the $290 million Anik E2 to operational status) as well as of non-space-weather-related events that can serve as proxies for disruptions caused by severe space storms (e.g., $4 billion to $10 billion for the power blackout of August 2003), and an estimate of $1 trillion to $2 trillion during the first year alone was given for the societal and economic costs of a "severe geomagnetic storm scenario" with recovery times of 4 to 10 years.

Such cost information is interesting and useful—but as the outcome of the workshop and this report make clear, it is at best only a starting point for the challenge of answering the question implicit in the title: What are the societal and economic impacts of severe space weather? To answer this question quantitatively, multiple variables must be taken into account, including the magnitude, duration, and timing of the event; the nature, severity, and extent of the collateral effects cascading through a society characterized by strong dependencies and interdependences; the robustness and resilience of the affected infrastructures; the risk management strategies and policies that the public and private sectors have in place; and the capability of the responsible federal, state, and local government agencies to respond to the effects of an extreme space weather event. While this workshop, along with its report, has gathered in one place much of what is currently known or suspected about societal and economic impacts, it has perhaps been most successful in illuminating the scope of the myriad issues involved, and the gaps in knowledge that remain to be explored in greater depth than can be accomplished in a workshop. A quantitative and comprehensive assessment of the societal and economic impacts of severe space weather will be a truly daunting task, and will involve questions that go well beyond the scope of the present report.

2

Fears of Damage from Solar Storms Are Overblown

Ian O'Neill

Ian O'Neill has a PhD in solar physics and has been writing for Universe Today, an astronomy news and community website, since 2007.

There are many stories that claim that the sun will doom planet Earth by unleashing killer solar flares that cripple the planet. Such fear-based hype is hogwash. The sun is stable and its behaviors are well known, and the Earth has safely survived for a very long time with the sun as its star. A solar storm's effect on Earth is highly dependent on such factors as the Earth's angle when a solar flare approaches; many times the event is unremarkable or simply produces an aurora of lights in the sky. Given the unreliability of the science for predicting solar storms, it is impossible to say whether the Earth will be affected by a solar flare at all, let alone one in a specific year. In the event that a strong solar flare does hit the Earth in a compromising way, satellites may sustain some damage and some electrical grids might be overwhelmed if they are not shut down preventatively beforehand, but nothing more serious than that will happen.

We could be in for a huge firework display in 2012. The Sun will be approaching the peak of its 11-year cycle, called "solar maximum", so we can expect a lot of solar activity. Some predictions put the solar maximum of Solar Cycle

24 even more energetic than the last solar maximum in 2002–2003. Solar physicists are already getting excited about this next cycle and new prediction methods are being put to good use. But should we be worried?

According to one of the many Doomsday scenarios we have been presented with in the run-up to the Mayan Prophecy-fuelled "end of the world" in the year 2012, this scenario is actually based on some science. What's more, there may be some correlation between the 11-year solar cycle and the time cycles seen in the Mayan calendar, perhaps this ancient civilization understood how the Sun's magnetism undergoes polarity changes every decade or so? Plus, religious texts (such as the Bible) say that we are due for a day of judgment, involving a lot of fire and brimstone. So it looks like we are going to get roasted alive by our closest star on December 21st, 2012!

Before we go jumping to conclusions, take a step back and think this through. Like most of the various ways the world is going to end in 2012, the possibility of the Sun blasting out a huge, Earth-damaging solar flare is very attractive to the doomsayers out there. But let's have a look at what really happens during an Earth-directed solar flare event: the Earth is actually very well protected. *Although some satellites may not be....*

The Earth has evolved in a highly radioactive environment. The Sun constantly fires high-energy particles from its magnetically dominated surface as the solar wind. During solar maximum (when the Sun is at its most active), the Earth may be unlucky enough to be staring down the barrel of an explosion with the energy of 100 billion Hiroshima-sized atomic bombs. This explosion is known as a solar flare, the effects of which can cause problems here on Earth.

Before we look at the Earth-side effects, let's have a look at the Sun and briefly understand why it gets so angry every 11 years or so.

The Sun's Natural Cycle

First and foremost, the Sun has a *natural* cycle with a period of approximately 11 years. During the lifetime of each cycle, the magnetic field lines of the Sun are dragged around the solar body by differential rotation at the solar equator. This means that the equator is spinning faster than the magnetic poles. As this continues, solar plasma drags the magnetic field lines around the Sun, causing stress and a build up of energy. As magnetic energy increases, kinks in the magnetic flux form, forcing them to the surface. These kinks are known as coronal loops which become more numerous during periods of high solar activity.

The biggest problem with an X-ray flare is that we get little warning when it is going to happen.

This is where the sunspots come in. As coronal loops continue to pop up over the surface, sunspots appear too, often located at the loop footpoints. Coronal loops have the effect of pushing the hotter surface layers of the Sun (the photosphere and chromosphere) aside, exposing the cooler convection zone (the reasons why the solar surface and atmosphere is hotter than the solar interior is down to the coronal heating phenomenon). As magnetic energy builds up, we can expect more and more magnetic flux to be forced together. This is when a phenomenon known as magnetic reconnection occurs.

Reconnection is the trigger for solar flares of various sizes. As previously reported, solar flares from "nanoflares" to "X-class flares" are very energetic events. Granted, the largest flares may generate enough energy for 100 billion atomic explosions, but don't let this huge figure concern you. For a start, this flare occurs in the low corona, right near the solar surface. That's nearly 100 million miles away (1AU). The Earth is nowhere close to the blast.

As the solar magnetic field lines release a huge amount of energy, solar plasma is accelerated and confined within the magnetic environment (solar plasma is superheated particles like protons, electrons and some light elements such as helium nuclei). As the plasma particles interact, X-rays may be generated if the conditions are right and *bremsstrahlung* is possible. (*Bremsstrahlung* occurs when charged particles interact, resulting in X-ray emission.) This may create an X-ray flare.

The Problem with X-ray Solar Flares

The biggest problem with an X-ray flare is that we get little warning when it is going to happen as X-rays travel at the speed of light. X-rays from an X-class flare will reach the Earth in around eight minutes. As X-rays hit our atmosphere, they are absorbed in the outermost layer called the ionosphere. As you can guess from the name, this is a highly charged, reactive environment, full of ions (atomic nuclei and free electrons).

Solar missions are actively working together to provide space agencies with advance notice of an Earth-directed [coronal mass ejection].

During powerful solar events such as flares, rates of ionization between X-rays and atmospheric gases increase in the D and E region layers of the ionosphere. There is a sudden surge in electron production in these layers. These electrons can cause interference to the passage of radio waves through the atmosphere, absorbing short wave radio signals (in the high frequency range), possibly blocking global communications. These events are known as "Sudden Ionospheric Disturbances" (or SIDs) and they become commonplace during periods of high solar activity. Interestingly, the increase in electron density during a SID boosts the propagation of Very

Low Frequency (VLF) radio, a phenomenon scientists use to measure the intensity of X-rays coming from the Sun.

Coronal Mass Ejection

X-ray solar flare emissions are only part of the story. If the conditions are right, a coronal mass ejection (CME) might be produced at the site of the flare (although either phenomenon can occur independently). CMEs are slower than the propagation of X-rays, but their global effects here on Earth can be more problematic. They may not travel at the speed of light, but they still travel fast; they can travel at a rate of 2 million miles per hour (3.2 million km/hr), meaning they may reach us in a matter of hours.

This is where much effort is being put into space weather prediction. We have a handful of spacecraft sitting between the Earth and the Sun at the Earth-Sun Lagrangian (L_1) point with sensors on board to measure the energy and intensity of the solar wind. Should a CME pass through their location, energetic particles and the interplanetary magnetic field (IMF) can be measured directly. One mission called the Advanced Composition Explorer (ACE) sits in the L_1 point and provides scientists with up to an hour notice on the approach of a CME. ACE teams up with the Solar and Heliospheric Observatory (SOHO) and the Solar TErrestrial RElations Observatory (STEREO), so CMEs can be tracked from the lower corona into interplanetary space, through the L_1 point toward Earth. These solar missions are actively working together to provide space agencies with advanced notice of an Earth-directed CME.

Alignment Matters

So what if a CME reaches Earth? For a start, much depends on the magnetic configuration of the IMF (from the Sun) and the geomagnetic field of the Earth (the magnetosphere). Generally speaking, if both magnetic fields are aligned with polarities pointing in the same direction, it is highly probable that the CME will be repelled by the magnetosphere. In this case, the CME will slide past the Earth, causing some pressure and distortion on the magnetosphere, but otherwise passing without a problem. However, if the magnetic field lines are in an anti-parallel configuration (i.e. magnetic polarities in opposite directions), magnetic reconnection may occur at the leading edge of the magnetosphere.

In this event, the IMF and magnetosphere will merge, connecting the Earth's magnetic field with the Sun's. This sets the scene for one of the most awe inspiring events in nature: the aurora.

Satellites in Peril

As the CME magnetic field connects with the Earth's, high energy particles are injected into the magnetosphere. Due to solar wind pressure, the Sun's magnetic field lines will fold around the Earth, sweeping behind our planet. The particles injected in the "dayside" will be funnelled into the polar regions of the Earth where they interact with our atmosphere, generating light as aurorae. During this time, the Van Allen belt [a belt of energetically charged particles, held in place by the Earth' magnetic field] will also become "super-charged", creating a region around the Earth that could cause problems to unprotected astronauts and any unshielded satellites. . . .

As if the radiation from the Van Allen belt wasn't enough, satellites could succumb to the threat of an expanding atmosphere. As you'd expect, if the Sun hits the Earth with X-rays and CMEs, there will be inevitable heating and global expansion of the atmosphere, possibly encroaching into satellite orbital altitudes. If left unchecked, an aerobraking effect on satellites could cause them to slow and drop in altitude. Aerobraking has been used extensively as a space flight *tool* to slow spacecraft down when being inserted into orbit around another planet, but this will have an adverse effect on satellites orbiting Earth as any slowing of velocity could cause it to re-enter the atmosphere.

Effects on the Ground

Although satellites are on the front line, if there is a powerful surge in energetic particles entering the atmosphere, we may feel the adverse effects down here on Earth too. Due to the X-ray generation of electrons in the ionosphere, some forms of communication may become patchy (or be removed all together), but this isn't all that can happen. Particularly in high-latitude regions, a vast electric current, known as an "electrojet", may form through the ionosphere by these incoming particles. With an electric current comes a magnetic field. Depending on the intensity of the solar storm, currents may be induced down here on the ground, possibly overloading national power grids. On March 13, 1989, six million people lost power in the Quebec region of Canada after a huge increase in solar activity caused a surge from ground-induced currents. Quebec was paralysed for nine hours whilst engineers worked on a solution to the problem.

Can Our Sun Produce a Killer Flare?

The short answer to this is "no".

The longer answer is a little more involved. Whilst a solar flare from our Sun, aimed directly at us, could cause secondary problems such as satellite damage and injury to unprotected astronauts and blackouts, the flare itself is not powerful enough to destroy Earth, certainly not in 2012. I dare say, in the far future when the Sun begins to run out of fuel and swell into a red giant, it might be a bad era for life on Earth, but we have a few billion years to wait for that to happen. There could even be the possibility of several X-class flares being launched and by pure bad luck we may get hit by a series of CMEs and X-ray bursts, but none will be powerful [enough] to overcome our magnetosphere, ionosphere and thick atmosphere below.

"Killer" solar flares *have* been observed on other stars. In 2006, NASA's Swift observatory saw the largest stellar flare ever observed 135 light-years away. Estimated to have unleashed an energy of 50 million *trillion* atomic bombs, the II Pegasi flare will have wiped out most life on Earth if our Sun fired X-rays from a flare of that energy at us. However, our Sun is not II Pegasi. II Pegasi is a violent red giant star with a binary partner in a very close orbit. It is believed the gravitational interaction with its binary partner and the fact II Pegasi is a red giant is the root cause behind this energetic flare event.

Regardless of prophesy, prediction or myth, there is no physical way to say that the Earth will be hit by any *flare, let alone a big one in 2012.*

Doomsayers point to the Sun as a possible Earth-killer source, but the fact remains that our Sun is a very stable star. It does not have a binary partner (like II Pegasi), it has a predictable cycle (of approximately 11 years) and there is no evidence that our Sun contributed to any mass extinction event in the past via a huge Earth-directed flare. Very large solar flares have been observed (such as the 1859 Carrington white light flare) . . . but we are still here.

Predictions Are Unreliable

In an added twist, solar physicists are surprised by the *lack* of solar activity at the start of this 24th solar cycle, leading some scientists to speculate we might be on the verge of another Maunder minimum and "Little Ice Age". This is in stark contrast to NASA solar physicist's 2006 prediction that this cycle will be a "doozy".

This leads me to conclude that we still have a long way to go when predicting solar flare events. Although space weather prediction is improving, it will be a few years yet until we can read the Sun accurately enough to say with any certainty just how active a solar cycle is going to be. So, regardless of prophecy, prediction or myth, there is no physical way to say that the Earth will be hit by *any* flare, let alone a big one in 2012. Even if a big flare did hit us, it will not be an extinction event. Yes, satellites may be damaged, causing secondary problems such as a GPS loss (which *might* disrupt air traffic control for example) or national power grids may be overwhelmed by auroral electrojets, but nothing more extreme than that.

3

A Solar Storm Could Cripple Communications and Power Grids Worldwide

Richard A. Lovett

Richard A. Lovett is a science writer based in Portland, Oregon. His work has appeared in Analog Science Fiction and Fact, Nature, New Scientist, *and* Psychology Today *magazines, among other publications. He is also a prolific science fiction writer.*

When the big solar storm known as the Carrington Event happened in 1859, the geomagnetic disturbance that hit the Earth was so strong that it lit up the sky and sent sparks shooting from telegraph machines, the main communications network of the day. If such a storm were to happen today, it could be devastating because modern society depends so heavily on electrical power and remote communications. Scientists say that the current eleven-year solar cycle may bring just such a storm and, if it does, the world's high-tech infrastructure could grind to a halt. Satellites, global positioning systems (GPS), and power grids are especially vulnerable and could all be knocked out by a big solar storm. Scientists are working to better predict solar storms in the hopes that advance warning will help prevent damage.

On February 14 [2011] the sun erupted with the largest solar flare seen in four years—big enough to interfere with radio communications and GPS [Global Positioning Systems] signals for airplanes on long-distance flights.

As solar storms go, the Valentine's Day flare was actually modest. But the burst of activity is only the start of the upcoming solar maximum, due to peak in the next couple of years.

"The sun has an activity cycle, much like hurricane season," Tom Bogdan, director of the Space Weather Prediction Center in Boulder, Colorado, said earlier this month [March 2011] at a meeting of the American Association for the Advancement of Science in Washington, D.C.

"It's been hibernating for four or five years, not doing much of anything." Now the sun is waking up, and even though the upcoming solar maximum may see a record low in the overall amount of activity, the individual events could be very powerful.

In fact, the biggest solar storm on record happened in 1859, during a solar maximum about the same size as the one we're entering, according to NASA [National Aeronautics and Space Administration].

That storm has been dubbed the Carrington Event, after British astronomer Richard Carrington, who witnessed the megaflare and was the first to realize the link between activity on the sun and geomagnetic disturbances on Earth.

The Carrington Event

During the Carrington Event, northern lights were reported as far south as Cuba and Honolulu, while southern lights were seen as far north as Santiago, Chile.

The flares were so powerful that "people in the northeastern U.S. could read newspaper print just from the light of the aurora," Daniel Baker, of the University of Colorado's Laboratory for Atmospheric and Space Physics, said at a geophysics meeting last December [2010].

In addition, the geomagnetic disturbances were strong enough that U.S. telegraph operators reported sparks leaping from their equipment—some bad enough to set fires, said Ed

Cliver, a space physicist at the U.S. Air Force Research Laboratory in Bedford, Massachusetts.

In 1859, such reports were mostly curiosities. But if something similar happened today, the world's high-tech infrastructure could grind to a halt.

"What's at stake," the Space Weather Prediction Center's Bogdan said, "are the advanced technologies that underlie virtually every aspect of our lives."

A Solar Flare Would Rupture Earth's "Cyber Cocoon"

To begin with, the University of Colorado's Baker said, electrical disturbances as strong as those that took down telegraph machines—"the Internet of the era"—would be far more disruptive.

Solar storms aimed at Earth come in three stages, not all of which occur in any given storm.

First, high-energy sunlight, mostly x-rays and ultraviolet light, ionizes Earth's upper atmosphere, interfering with radio communications. Next comes a radiation storm, potentially dangerous to unprotected astronauts.

Finally comes a coronal mass ejection, or CME, a slower moving cloud of charged particles that can take several days to reach Earth's atmosphere. When a CME hits, the solar particles can interact with Earth's magnetic field to produce powerful electromagnetic fluctuations.

"We live in a cyber cocoon enveloping the Earth," Baker said. "Imagine what the consequences might be."

Of particular concern are disruptions to global positioning systems (GPS), which have become ubiquitous in cell phones, airplanes, and automobiles, Baker said. A $13 billion business in 2003, the GPS industry is predicted to grow to nearly $1 trillion by 2017.

In addition, Baker said, satellite communications—also essential to many daily activities—would be at risk from solar storms.

"Every time you purchase a gallon of gas with your credit card, that's a satellite transaction," he said.

The eastern half of the U.S. is particularly vulnerable, because the power infrastructure is highly interconnected, so failures could easily cascade like chains of dominoes.

Fears Center on Power Grid

But the big fear is what might happen to the electrical grid, since power surges caused by solar particles could blow out giant transformers. Such transformers can take a long time to replace, especially if hundreds are destroyed at once, said Baker, who is a co-author of a National Research Council report on solar-storm risks.

The U.S. Air Force Research Laboratory's Cliver agrees: "They don't have a lot of these on the shelf," he said.

The eastern half of the U.S. is particularly vulnerable, because the power infrastructure is highly interconnected, so failures could easily cascade like chains of dominoes.

"Imagine large cities without power for a week, a month, or a year," Baker said. "The losses could be $1 to $2 trillion, and the effects could be felt for years."

Even if the latest solar maximum doesn't bring a Carrington-level event, smaller storms have been known to affect power and communications.

The "Halloween storms" of 2003, for instance, interfered with satellite communications, produced a brief power outage in Sweden, and lighted up the skies with ghostly auroras as far south as Florida and Texas.

Buffing Up Space-Weather Predictions

One solution is to rebuild the aging power grid to be less vulnerable to solar disruptions.

Another is better forecasting. Scientists using the new Solar Dynamics Observatory spacecraft are hoping to get a better understanding of how the sun behaves as it moves deeper into its next maximum and begins generating bigger storms.

These studies may help scientists predict when and where solar flares might appear and whether a given storm is pointed at Earth.

"Improved predictions will provide more accurate forecasts, so [officials] can take mitigating actions," said Rodney Viereck, a physicist at the Space Weather Prediction Center.

Scientists are scrambling to learn everything they can about the sun in an effort to produce even longer-range forecasts.

Even now, the center's Bogdan said, the most damaging emissions from big storms travel slowly enough to be detected by sun-watching satellites well before the particles strike Earth. "That gives us [about] 20 hours to determine what actions we need to take," Viereck said.

In a pinch, power companies could protect valuable transformers by taking them offline before the storm strikes. That would produce local blackouts, but they wouldn't last for long.

"The good news is that these storms tend to pass after a couple of hours," Bogdan added.

Meanwhile, scientists are scrambling to learn everything they can about the sun in an effort to produce even longer-range forecasts.

According to Viereck, space-weather predictions have some catching up to do: "We're back where weather forecasters were 50 years ago."

4

The Current Solar Storm Cycle Will Be Milder than Thought

National Oceanic and Atmospheric Administration (NOAA)

The National Oceanic and Atmospheric Administration (NOAA), pronounced "noah," is a scientific agency within the United States Department of Commerce that focuses on the conditions of the oceans and the atmosphere.

The National Oceanic and Atmospheric Administration's (NOAA) Space Weather Prediction Center reports that Solar Cycle 24—which is under way now and expected to peak in May 2013—will not be as strong as previously believed. Based on observing less-than-anticipated sunspot activity, NOAA revised its 2007 prediction of a strong cycle and now says that it could actually be the weakest cycle since 1928. Fewer sunspots mean less chance of a solar storm, but such a prediction is not a guarantee. Although experts see a diminished chance of a major solar storm zapping the world's satellites, communications networks, and power grids in the next couple years, a solar storm could still happen at any time and the high-tech infrastructure of the modern world remains highly vulnerable to severe damage from its effects.

Although its peak is still [a few] years away [2013] a new active period of Earth-threatening solar storms will be the weakest since 1928, predicts an international panel of experts

"Mild Solar Storm Season Predicted," National Oceanic and Atmospheric Administration (NOAA), May 8, 2009.

led by NOAA's [the National Oceanic and Atmospheric Administration] Space Weather Prediction Center and funded by NASA [National Aeronautics and Space Administration]. Despite the prediction, Earth is still vulnerable to a severe solar storm.

Solar storms are eruptions of energy and matter that escape from the sun and may head toward Earth, where even a weak storm can damage satellites and power grids, disrupting communications, the electric power supply and GPS. A single strong blast of "solar wind" can threaten national security, transportation, financial services and other essential functions.

The more sunspots there are, the more likely it is that solar storms will occur.

The panel predicts the upcoming Solar Cycle 24 will peak in May 2013 with 90 sunspots per day on average. If the prediction proves true, Solar Cycle 24 will be the weakest cycle since number 16, which peaked at 78 daily suns pots in 1928, and ninth weakest since the 1750s, when numbered cycles began.

The most common measure of a solar cycle's intensity is the number of sunspots—Earth-sized blotches on the sun marking areas of heightened magnetic activity. The more sunspots there are, the more likely it is that solar storms will occur, but a major storm can occur at anytime.

"As with hurricanes, whether a cycle is active or weak refers to the number of storms, but everyone needs to remember it only takes one powerful storm to cause huge problems," said NOAA scientist Doug Biesecker, who chairs the panel. "The strongest solar storm on record occurred in 1859 during another below-average cycle."

The 1859 storm shorted out telegraph wires, causing fires in North America and Europe, sent readings of Earth's magnetic field soaring, and produced northern lights so bright that people read newspapers by their light.

A recent report by the National Academy of Sciences found that if a storm that severe occurred today, it could cause $1–2 trillion in damages the first year and require four to 10 years for recovery, compared to $80–125 billion that resulted from Hurricane Katrina.

Revising the Prediction

The panel also predicted that the lowest sunspot number between cycles—or solar minimum—occurred in December 2008, marking the end of Cycle 23 and the start of Cycle 24. If the December prediction holds up, at 12 years and seven months Solar Cycle 23 will be the longest since 1823 and the third longest since 1755. Solar cycles span 11 years on average, from minimum to minimum.

Today every hiccup from the sun aimed at Earth has potential consequences.

An unusually long, deep lull in sunspots led the panel to revise its 2007 prediction that the next cycle of solar storms would start in March 2008 and peak in late 2011 or mid-2012. The persistence of a quiet sun also led the panel to a consensus that the next cycle will be "moderately weak."

NOAA's Space Weather Prediction Center (SWPC) is the nation's first alert of solar activity and its effects on Earth. The Center's space weather experts issue outlooks for the next 11-year solar cycle and warn of storms occurring on the Sun that could impact Earth. SWPC is also the world warning agency for the International Space Environment Service, a consortium of 12 member nations.

As the world economy becomes more reliant on satellite-based communications and interlinked power grids, interest in solar activity has grown dramatically. In 2008 alone, SWPC acquired 1,700 new subscription customers for warnings, alerts, reports, and other products. Among the new customers are emergency managers, airlines, state transportation departments, oil companies, and nuclear power stations. SWPC's customers reside in 150 countries.

"Our customer growth reflects today's reality that all sectors of society are highly dependent on advanced, space-based technologies," said SWPC director Tom Bogdan. "Today every hiccup from the sun aimed at Earth has potential consequences."

5

Solar Storm Predictions Needlessly Inflame 2012 Doomsday Fears

Alan Boyle

Alan Boyle is the science editor at msnbc.com. He is the author of The Case for Pluto, *and his msnbc.com blog, "Cosmic Log," won the National Academies Communication Award in 2008.*

It is a good idea to apply some measured reason to the doomsday predictions concerning the end of the world in 2012, according to the ancient Mayan calendar. While it is true that solar storms could play havoc with the Earth's communications and power systems in roughly the same time period, it is no reason to panic, and it will certainly not be a doomsday scenario—Mayan or otherwise. While a solar storm could indeed disrupt satellites and cause black-outs from power-grid failures, it is not the end of the world. The impact of a solar storm would be inconvenient rather than life-threatening. Individuals should be prepared to be self-sufficient when such an event happens, however. Always having an emergency supply of food, water, medicine, and other essentials on hand is a good idea in order to be prepared for natural disasters of any kind.

Don't panic over those reports that solar storms could cause high-tech disruptions in 2013. But don't ignore them either. That's the word from NASA Headquarters' top guy for solar science.

Concerns about the potential for an unprecedented assault from space were stoked last week [June 2010] by a report in London's *Telegraph*, warning that a super storm could cause "catastrophic consequences for the world's health, emergency services and national security unless precautions are taken."

Amid all the hype about a 2012 Maya apocalypse, there's been increasing talk about the potential for a solar super-storm.

The warnings focus on the 2012–2013 time frame, because that's when the 11-year solar activity cycle is expected to peak. Back in 2006, solar scientists said the coming peak, known as solar maximum or "solar max," could be 30 to 50 percent stronger than the last one, based on a computer model that looked at how plasma circulates between the sun's equator and its poles.

Since then, additional reports have added to the concern: In 2008, a National Academy of Sciences study said a severe geomagnetic storm could cause $2 trillion in damage and require as much as a decade of recovery time. In comparison, the damage estimate for Hurricane Katrina [in 2005] is a mere $80 billion or so.

Assessing the Hype

Amid all the hype about a 2012 Maya apocalypse, there's been increasing talk about the potential for a solar superstorm on the scale of 1859's "Carrington event," which shorted out telegraph wires, sparked fires and set off auroral displays as far south as Cuba. The fear is that the damage would be more severe in this world of GPS navigation, satellite communications and mobile devices.

The *Telegraph*'s article quoted Richard Fisher, the head of NASA's Heliospheric Division at the space agency's Washington headquarters, as saying that a superstorm would "cause major problems for the world."

"It will disrupt communication devices such as satellites and car navigation, air travel, the banking system, our computers, everything that is electronic," he told the *Telegraph*.

When I caught up with Fisher, his forecast was less dire, and less definite: He told me it's far too early to say just how strong the next solar maximum will be. In fact, some experts are now predicting that the intensity will be well below average, based on the fact that the sun has been unusually quiet in recent years.

"The next maximum is anticipated to be somewhere around the lowest ever seen to a little bit higher than the highest that's ever been seen," Fisher said half-jokingly. "I think it was Yogi Berra who said . . . the problem with predictions is that they all take place in the future."

Disruption Is No Joke

But Fisher doesn't joke about the need to be prepared for the potential disruptions caused by space weather. A bad solar storm could easily have a negative impact on everyday life. For example, air traffic over the North Pole has increased dramatically since the previous solar maximum in 2001. If severe geomagnetic storms were to sweep past Earth, those flights would have to be shifted farther south to guard against communication disruptions. This year's Icelandic ash mess [the May 2011 eruption of the Grímsvötn volcano in Iceland] suggests how a situation like that might affect global travel and commerce.

"It has a fairly large economic impact on an airline if you have to divert an airliner," Fisher noted.

Fortunately, the methods for predicting space weather have improved over the past decade or two. Satellites such as the Advanced Composition Explorer can spot the signs of a geomagnetic storm up to an hour before it hits our planet, providing valuable lead time for power grid operators. (A space storm in 1989 sparked a nine-hour electrical blackout in Quebec, affecting 6 million customers and costing the power company more than $10 million.) Other observing instruments, which measure seismic activity originating on the far side of the sun, can provide a couple of weeks of warning about active sunspot regions.

"Be Prepared" Is a Good Motto

So how bad does Fisher think things can get in 2013?

"I think there's a relatively high probability that there will be a solar event that will have some effect over hours to tens of hours. That's pretty high in the next 10 years," he told me. "I think that it's a low probability but a very high-impact circumstance for a large solar event that disrupts infrastructure for periods of longer than a day or two."

He doesn't advise preparing for Armageddon, but he does suggest that you have an emergency supply of food, water and the other things you need to weather a disaster. Which is good advice whether or not a superstorm hits in 2013.

"In modern life, you want to understand how vulnerable you are," Fisher said. "A good big winter storm will knock out the local power delivery for hours to a day or two. I keep a little water around the house in case that situation happens. There are alternate systems for providing power to hospitals, critical records and things like that. I think it'll be inconvenient, as opposed to ... well, not necessarily *deadly*, for goodness' sake."

6

Global Recovery from a Solar Storm Could Take Years

Michael Brooks

Michael Brooks is a quantum physicist and former editor of New Scientist *magazine. His science articles have appeared in numerous publications around the world, and he is the author of several books.*

A recent report on the potential consequence of a severe solar storm, done by the National Aeronautics and Space Administration (NASA) and the US National Academy of Sciences (NAS), is frightening. The report envisions a global disaster of epic proportions if the Earth's high-tech infrastructure is zapped by geomagnetic storm activity from the sun, and it concludes that such an event is not unlikely. Especially vulnerable are the world's power grids; more than one hundred and thirty million people could be without power long-term if such an event were to occur. It could take years to manufacture and replace the large number of electrical transformers around the world. Meanwhile, people would struggle to survive without heating, cooling, refrigeration, transportation, communications, banking, and so forth. NAS estimates the recovery time at four to ten years, and the economic cost could be in the trillions in the first year alone.

It is midnight on 22 September 2012, and the skies above Manhattan are filled with a flickering curtain of colourful light. Few New Yorkers have seen the aurora this far south but their fascination is short-lived. Within a few seconds, electric bulbs dim and flicker, then become unusually bright for a fleeting moment. Then all the lights in the state go out. Within 90 seconds, the entire eastern half of the U.S. is without power.

A year later and millions of Americans are dead and the nation's infrastructure lies in tatters. The World Bank declares America a developing nation. Europe, Scandinavia, China and Japan are also struggling to recover from the same fateful event—a violent storm, 150 million kilometres away on the surface of the sun.

We're moving closer and closer to the edge of a possible disaster.

It sounds ridiculous. Surely the sun couldn't create so profound a disaster on Earth. Yet an extraordinary report funded by NASA and issued by the US National Academy of Sciences (NAS) in January [2009] claims it could do just that.

Over the last few decades, western civilisations have busily sown the seeds of their own destruction. Our modern way of life, with its reliance on technology, has unwittingly exposed us to an extraordinary danger: plasma balls spewed from the surface of the sun could wipe out our power grids, with catastrophic consequences.

The projections of just how catastrophic make chilling reading. "We're moving closer and closer to the edge of a possible disaster," says Daniel Baker, a space weather expert based at the University of Colorado in Boulder, and chair of the NAS committee responsible for the report.

The Sun's Mechanics

It is hard to conceive of the sun wiping out a large amount of our hard-earned progress. Nevertheless, it is possible. The surface of the sun is a roiling mass of plasma—charged high-energy particles—some of which escape the surface and travel through space as the solar wind. From time to time, that wind carries a billion-tonne glob of plasma, a fireball known as a coronal mass ejection. If one should hit the Earth's magnetic shield, the result could be truly devastating.

The incursion of the plasma into our atmosphere causes rapid changes in the configuration of Earth's magnetic field which, in turn, induce currents in the long wires of the power grids. The grids were not built to handle this sort of direct current electricity. The greatest danger is at the step-up and step-down transformers used to convert power from its transport voltage to domestically useful voltage. The increased DC current creates strong magnetic fields that saturate a transformer's magnetic core. The result is runaway current in the transformer's copper wiring, which rapidly heats up and melts. This is exactly what happened in the Canadian province of Quebec in March 1989, and six million people spent 9 hours without electricity. But things could get much, much worse than that.

The Carrington Event Is the Benchmark

The most serious space weather event in history happened in 1859. It is known as the Carrington event, after the British amateur astronomer Richard Carrington, who was the first to note its cause: "two patches of intensely bright and white light" emanating from a large group of sunspots. The Carrington event comprised eight days of severe space weather.

There were eyewitness accounts of stunning auroras, even at equatorial latitudes. The world's telegraph networks experienced severe disruptions, and Victorian magnetometers were driven off the scale.

Though a solar outburst could conceivably be more powerful, "we haven't found an example of anything worse than a Carrington event", says James Green, head of NASA's planetary division and an expert on the events of 1859. "From a scientific perspective, that would be the one that we'd want to survive." However, the prognosis from the NAS analysis is that, thanks to our technological prowess, many of us may not.

There are two problems to face. The first is the modern electricity grid, which is designed to operate at ever higher voltages over ever larger areas. Though this provides a more efficient way to run the electricity networks, minimising power losses and wastage through overproduction, it has made them much more vulnerable to space weather. The high-power grids act as particularly efficient antennas, channelling enormous direct currents into the power transformers.

Usually the less developed regions of the world are most vulnerable, not the highly sophisticated technological regions.

The second problem is the grid's interdependence with the systems that support our lives: water and sewage treatment, supermarket delivery infrastructures, power station controls, financial markets and many others all rely on electricity. Put the two together, and it is clear that a repeat of the Carrington event could produce a catastrophe the likes of which the world has never seen. "It's just the opposite of how we usually think of natural disasters," says John Kappenman, a power industry analyst with the Metatech Corporation of Goleta, California, and an advisor to the NAS committee that produced the report. "Usually the less developed regions of the world are most vulnerable, not the highly sophisticated technological regions."

The Clock Starts Ticking

According to the NAS report, a severe space weather event in the US could induce ground currents that would knock out 300 key transformers within about 90 seconds, cutting off the power for more than 130 million people. From that moment, the clock is ticking for America.

First to go—immediately for some people—is drinkable water. Anyone living in a high-rise apartment, where water has to be pumped to reach them, would be cut off straight away. For the rest, drinking water will still come through the taps for maybe half a day. With no electricity to pump water from reservoirs, there is no more after that.

There is simply no electrically powered transport: no trains, underground or overground. Our just-in-time culture for delivery networks may represent the pinnacle of efficiency, but it means that supermarket shelves would empty very quickly—delivery trucks could only keep running until their tanks ran out of fuel, and there is no electricity to pump any more from the underground tanks at filling stations.

Back-up generators would run at pivotal sites—but only until their fuel ran out. For hospitals, that would mean about 72 hours of running a bare-bones, essential care only, service. After that, no more modern healthcare.

Recovery Would Take Time

The truly shocking finding is that this whole situation would not improve for months, maybe years: melted transformer hubs cannot be repaired, only replaced. "From the surveys I've done, you might have a few spare transformers around, but installing a new one takes a well-trained crew a week or more," says Kappenman. "A major electrical utility might have one suitably trained crew, maybe two."

Those willing to help are likely to be ill-equipped to deal with the sheer scale of the disaster.

Within a month, then, the handful of spare transformers would be used up. The rest will have to be built to order, something that can take up to 12 months.

Even when some systems are capable of receiving power again, there is no guarantee there will be any to deliver. Almost all natural gas and fuel pipelines require electricity to operate. Coal-fired power stations usually keep reserves to last 30 days, but with no transport systems running to bring more fuel, there will be no electricity in the second month.

Nuclear power stations wouldn't fare much better. They are programmed to shut down in the event of serious grid problems and are not allowed to restart until the power grid is up and running.

Lives in Jeopardy

With no power for heating, cooling or refrigeration systems, people could begin to die within days. There is immediate danger for those who rely on medication. Lose power to New Jersey, for instance, and you have lost a major centre of production of pharmaceuticals for the entire US. Perishable medications such as insulin will soon be in short supply. "In the US alone there are a million people with diabetes," Kappenman says. "Shut down production, distribution and storage and you put all those lives at risk in very short order."

It is questionable whether the US would ever bounce back.

Help is not coming any time soon, either. If it is dark from the eastern seaboard to Chicago, some affected areas are hundreds, maybe thousands of miles away from anyone who might help. And those willing to help are likely to be ill-equipped to deal with the sheer scale of the disaster. "If a Carrington event happened now, it would be like a hurricane Katrina [2005 Gulf Coast, US] but 10 times worse," says Paul Kintner, a plasma physicist at Cornell University in Ithaca, New York.

In reality, it would be much worse than that. Hurricane Katrina's societal and economic impact has been measured at $81 billion to $125 billion. According to the NAS report, the impact of what it terms a "severe geomagnetic storm scenario" could be as high as $2 trillion. And that's just the first year after the storm. The NAS puts the recovery time at four to 10 years. It is questionable whether the US would ever bounce back.

The Whole World Is Vulnerable

"I don't think the NAS report is scaremongering," says Mike Hapgood, who chairs the European Space Agency's space weather team. Green agrees. "Scientists are conservative by nature and this group is really thoughtful," he says. "This is a fair and balanced report."

Such nightmare scenarios are not restricted to North America. High latitude nations such as Sweden and Norway have been aware for a while that, while regular views of the aurora are pretty, they are also reminders of an ever-present threat to their electricity grids. However, the trend towards installing extremely high voltage grids means that lower latitude countries are also at risk. For example, China is on the way to implementing a 1000-kilovolt electrical grid, twice the voltage of the US grid. This would be a superb conduit for space weather-induced disaster because the grid's efficiency to act as an antenna rises as the voltage between the grid and the ground increases. "China is going to discover at some point that they have a problem," Kappenman says.

Neither is Europe sufficiently prepared. Responsibility for dealing with space weather issues is "very fragmented" in Europe, says Hapgood.

Europe's electricity grids, on the other hand, are highly interconnected and extremely vulnerable to cascading failures. In 2006, the routine switch-off of a small part of Germany's grid—to let a ship pass safely under high-voltage cables— caused a cascade power failure across western Europe. In France alone, five million people were left without electricity for two hours. "These systems are so complicated we don't fully understand the effects of twiddling at one place," Hapgood says. "Most of the time it's alright, but occasionally it will get you."

The Warning Systems Are Unreliable

The good news is that, given enough warning, the utility companies can take precautions, such as adjusting voltages and loads, and restricting transfers of energy so that sudden spikes in current don't cause cascade failures. There is still more bad news, however. Our early warning system is becoming more unreliable by the day.

By far the most important indicator of incoming space weather is NASA's Advanced Composition Explorer (ACE). The probe, launched in 1997, has a solar orbit that keeps it directly between the sun and Earth. Its uninterrupted view of the sun means it gives us continuous reports on the direction and velocity of the solar wind and other streams of charged particles that flow past its sensors. ACE can provide between 15 and 45 minutes' warning of any incoming geomagnetic storms. The power companies need about 15 minutes to prepare their systems for a critical event, so that would seem passable.

If policy-makers show a similar indifference in the face of the latest NAS report, it could cost tens of millions of lives.

The ACE Probe May Fail

However, observations of the sun and magnetometer readings during the Carrington event shows that the coronal mass ejection was travelling so fast it took less than 15 minutes to get from where ACE is positioned to Earth. "It arrived faster than we can do anything," Hapgood says.

There is another problem. ACE is 11 years old, and operating well beyond its planned lifespan. The onboard detectors are not as sensitive as they used to be, and there is no telling when they will finally give up the ghost. Furthermore, its sensors become saturated in the event of a really powerful solar flare. "It was built to look at average conditions rather than extremes," Baker says.

He was part of a space weather commission that three years ago [2006] warned about the problems of relying on ACE. "It's been on my mind for a long time," he says. "To not have a spare, or a strategy to replace it if and when it should fail, is rather foolish."

There is no replacement for ACE due any time soon. Other solar observation satellites, such as the Solar and Heliospheric Observatory (SOHO) can provide some warning, but with less detailed information and—crucially—much later. "It's quite hard to assess what the impact of losing ACE will be," Hapgood says. "We will largely lose the early warning capability."

"Deep Indifference"

The world will, most probably, yawn at the prospect of a devastating solar storm until it happens. Kintner says his students show a "deep indifference" when he lectures on the impact of space weather. But if policy-makers show a similar indifference in the face of the latest NAS report, it could cost tens of millions of lives, Kappenman reckons. "It could conceivably be the worst natural disaster possible," he says.

The report outlines the worst case scenario for the US. The "perfect storm" is most likely on a spring or autumn night in a year of heightened solar activity—something like 2012. Around the equinoxes, the orientation of the Earth's field to the sun makes us particularly vulnerable to a plasma strike.

What's more, at these times of year, electricity demand is relatively low because no one needs too much heating or air conditioning. With only a handful of the US grid's power stations running, the system relies on computer algorithms shunting large amounts of power around the grid and this leaves the network highly vulnerable to sudden spikes.

If ACE has failed by then, or a plasma ball flies at us too fast for any warning from ACE to reach us, the consequences could be staggering. "A really large storm could be a planetary disaster," Kappenman says.

Little Momentum on Solutions

So what should be done? No one knows yet—the report is meant to spark that conversation. Baker is worried, though, that the odds are stacked against that conversation really getting started. As the NAS report notes, it is terribly difficult to inspire people to prepare for a potential crisis that has never happened before and may not happen for decades to come. "It takes a lot of effort to educate policy-makers, and that is especially true with these low-frequency events," he says.

We should learn the lessons of Hurricane Katrina, though, and realise that "unlikely" doesn't mean "won't happen". Especially when the stakes are so high. The fact is, it could come in the next three or four years—and with devastating effects. "The Carrington event happened during a mediocre, ho-hum solar cycle," Kintner says. "It came out of nowhere, so we just don't know when something like that is going to happen again."

7

Bracing the Satellite Infrastructure for a Solar Superstorm

Sten F. Odenwald and James L. Green

*Sten F. Odenwald is a National Aeronautics and Space Adminis-
tration (NASA) astronomer who researches the economic impacts of solar "superstorms" on the commercial satellite network.
He runs the Astronomy Café website and is the author of several
books. James L. Green is director of the Planetary Science Division at NASA's Science Mission Directorate.*

*To understand how severely a solar "superstorm" would impact
our modern-day technological infrastructure, scientists are looking closely at the largest solar storm on record, the Carrington
Event of 1859. Researchers have broken that storm, and others
like it, down into several unique phases of solar activity, each of
which produces its own unique effects on the Earth and its atmosphere. By knowing exactly what types of solar phenomena
account for which effects, scientists hope to learn how to identify
specific vulnerabilities in such technologies as satellites and power
delivery systems. Identifying the vulnerabilities is the first step
toward finding ways to strengthen modern technologies against a
future solar storm, but much work remains to be done. In order
to learn how to protect effectively the modern-day technological*

Sten F. Odenwald and James L. Green, "Bracing the Satellite Infrastructure for a Solar
Superstorm," *Scientific American*, July 28, 2008. Originally published by Scientific American, Inc. Copyright © 2008 by Scientific American. All rights reserved. Reproduced by
permission.

infrastructure, more money must be spent on research so that scientists can learn to better forecast solar storms and model their potential impact.

As night was falling across the Americas on Sunday, August 28, 1859, the phantom shapes of the auroras could already be seen overhead. From Maine to the tip of Florida, vivid curtains of light took the skies. Startled Cubans saw the auroras directly overhead; ships' logs near the equator described crimson lights reaching halfway to the zenith. Many people thought their cities had caught fire. Scientific instruments around the world, patiently recording minute changes in Earth's magnetism, suddenly shot off scale, and spurious electric currents surged into the world's telegraph systems. In Baltimore telegraph operators labored from 8 p.m. until 10 a.m. the next day to transmit a mere 400-word press report.

Just before noon the following Thursday, September 1, English astronomer Richard C. Carrington was sketching a curious group of sunspots—curious on account of the dark areas' enormous size. At 11:18 a.m. he witnessed an intense white light flash from two locations within the sunspot group. He called out in vain to anyone in the observatory to come see the brief five-minute spectacle, but solitary astronomers seldom have an audience to share their excitement. Seventeen hours later in the Americas a second wave of auroras turned night to day as far south as Panama. People could read the newspaper by their crimson and green light. Gold miners in the Rocky Mountains woke up and ate breakfast at 1 a.m., thinking the sun had risen on a cloudy day. Telegraph systems became unusable across Europe and North America.

The news media of the day looked for researchers able to explain the phenomena, but at the time scientists scarcely understood auroral displays at all. Were they meteoritic matter from space, reflected light from polar icebergs or a high-altitude version of lightning? It was the Great Aurora of 1859 itself that ushered in a new paradigm. The October 15 issue of

Scientific American noted that "a connection between the northern lights and forces of electricity and magnetism is now fully established." Work since then has established that auroral displays ultimately originate in violent events on the sun, which fire off huge clouds of plasma and momentarily disrupt our planet's magnetic field.

Coronal mass ejections (CMEs) are analogous to hurricanes; they are giant magnetic bubbles, millions of kilometers across, that hurl billion-ton plasma clouds into space.

The impact of the 1859 storm was muted only by the infancy of our technological civilization at that time. Were it to happen today, it could severely damage satellites, disable radio communications and cause continent-wide electrical blackouts that would require weeks or longer to recover from. Although a storm of that magnitude is a comfortably rare once-in-500-years event, those with half its intensity hit every 50 years or so. The last one, which occurred on November 13, 1960, led to worldwide geomagnetic disturbances and radio outages. If we make no preparations, by some calculations the direct and indirect costs of another superstorm could equal that of a major hurricane or earthquake.

The Big One

The number of sunspots, along with other signs of solar magnetic activity, waxes and wanes on an 11-year cycle. The current cycle began this past January [2008]; over the coming half a decade, solar activity will ramp up from its current lull. During the previous 11 years, 21,000 flares and 13,000 clouds of ionized gas, or plasma, exploded from the sun's surface. These phenomena, collectively termed solar storms, arise from the relentless churning of solar gases. In some ways, they are scaled-up versions of terrestrial storms, with the important difference that magnetic fields lace the solar gases that sculpt and energize them. Flares are analogous to lightning storms; they are bursts of energetic particles and intense x-rays resulting from changes in the magnetic field on a relatively small scale by the sun's standards, spanning thousands of kilometers. So-called coronal mass ejections (CMEs) are analogous to hurricanes; they are giant magnetic bubbles, millions of kilometers across, that hurl billion-ton plasma clouds into space at several million kilometers per hour.

Most of these storms result in nothing more than auroras dancing in the polar skies—the equivalent of a minor afternoon rainstorm on Earth. Occasionally, however, the sun lets loose a gale. No one living today has ever experienced a full-blown superstorm, but telltale signs of them have turned up in some surprising places. In ice-core data from Greenland and Antarctica, Kenneth G. McCracken of the University of Maryland has discovered sudden jumps in the concentration of trapped nitrate gases, which in recent decades appear to correlate with known blasts of solar particles. A nitrate anomaly found for 1859 stands out as the biggest of the past 500 years, with the severity roughly equivalent to the sum of all the major events of the past 40 years.

As violent as it was, the 1859 superstorm does not appear to have been qualitatively different from lesser events. The two of us, along with many other researchers, have reconstructed what happened back then from contemporary historical accounts as well as scaled-up measurements of milder storms in recent decades, which have been studied by modern satellites:

1. **The gathering storm.** On the sun, the preconditions for the 1859 superstorm involved the appearance of a large, near-equatorial sunspot group around the peak of the sunspot cycle. The sunspots were so large that astronomers such as Carrington could see them with the naked (but suitably protected) eye. At the time of the initial CME released by the storm, this sunspot group was op-

posite Earth, putting our planet squarely in the bull's-eye. The sun's aim need not be so exact, however. By the time a CME reaches Earth's orbit, it typically has fanned out to a width of some 50 million kilometers, thousands of times wider than our planet.

2. **First blast**. The superstorm released not one but two CMEs. The first may have taken the customary 40 to 60 hours to arrive. The magnetometer data from 1859 suggest that the magnetic field in the ejected plasma probably had a helical shape. When it first hit Earth, the field was pointing north. In this orientation, the field reinforced Earth's own magnetic field, which minimized its effects. The CME did compress Earth's magnetosphere—the region of near-Earth space where our planet's magnetic field dominates the sun's—and registered at magnetometer stations on the ground as what solar scientists call a sudden storm commencement. Otherwise it went unnoticed. As plasma continued to stream past Earth, however, its field slowly spun around. After 15 hours, it opposed rather than reinforced Earth's field, bringing our planet's north-pointing and the plasma cloud's south-pointing field lines into contact. The field lines then reconnected into a simpler shape, releasing huge amounts of stored energy. That is when the telegraph disruptions and auroral displays commenced. Within a day or two the plasma passed by Earth, and our planet's geomagnetic field returned to normal.

3. **X-ray flare**. The largest CMEs typically coincide with one or more intense flares, and the 1859 superstorm was no exception. The visible flare observed by Carrington and others on September 1 implied temperatures of nearly 50 million kelvins. Accordingly, it probably emitted not only visible light but also x-rays and gamma rays. It was the most brilliant solar flare ever recorded,

bespeaking enormous energies released into the solar atmosphere. The radiation hit Earth after the light travel time of eight and a half minutes, long before the second CME. Had shortwave radios existed, they would have been rendered useless by energy deposition in the iono-sphere, the high-altitude layer of ionized gas that reflects radio waves. The x-ray energy also heated the upper atmosphere and caused it to bloat out by tens or hun-dreds of kilometers.

4. **Second blast**. Before the ambient solar-wind plasma had time to fill in the cavity formed by the passage of the first CME, the sun fired off a second CME. With little material to impede it, the CME reached Earth within 17 hours. This time the CME field pointed south as it hit, and the geomagnetic mayhem was immediate. Such was its violence that it compressed Earth's magnetosphere (which usually extends about 60,000 kilometers) to 7,000 kilometers or perhaps even into the upper strato-sphere itself. The Van Allen radiation belts that encircle our planet were temporarily eliminated, and huge num-bers of protons and electrons were dumped into the upper atmosphere. These particles may have accounted for the intense red auroras seen in much of the world.

5. **Energetic protons**. The solar flare and the intense CMEs also accelerated protons to energies of 30 million elec-tron volts or higher. Across the Arctic, where Earth's magnetic field affords the least protection, these particles penetrated to an altitude of 50 kilometers and deposited additional energy in the ionosphere. According to Brian C. Thomas of Washburn University, the proton shower from the 1859 superstorm reduced stratospheric ozone by 5 percent. The layer took four years to recover. The most powerful protons, with energies above one billion electron volts, reacted with the nuclei of nitrogen and

oxygen atoms in the air, spawning neutrons and creating the nitrate abundance anomalies. A rain of neutrons reached the ground in what is now called a ground level event, but no human technology was available to detect this onslaught. Fortunately, it was not hazardous to health.

6. **Massive electric currents.** As the auroras spread from the usual high latitudes to low latitudes, the accompanying ionospheric and auroral electric currents induced intense, continent-spanning currents in the ground. These currents found their way into telegraph circuitry. The multiampere, high-voltage discharges caused near electrocutions and were reported to have burned down several telegraph stations.

Toasted Satellites

When a large geomagnetic storm happens again, the most obvious victims will be satellites. Even under ordinary conditions, cosmic-ray particles erode solar panels and reduce power generation by about 2 percent annually. Incoming particles also interfere with satellite electronics. Many communications satellites, such as Anik E1 and E2 in 1994 and Telstar 401 in 1997, have been compromised or lost in this way. A large solar storm can cause one to three years' worth of satellite lifetime loss in a matter of hours and produce hundreds of glitches, ranging from errant but harmless commands to destructive electrostatic discharges.

To see how communications satellites might fare, we simulated 1,000 ways a superstorm might unfold, with intensities that varied from the worst storm of the Space Age (which occurred on October 20, 1989) to that of the 1859 superstorm. We found that the storms would not only degrade solar panels as expected but also lead to the significant loss of transponder revenue. The total cost would often exceed $20 billion. We assumed that satellite owners and designers would have mitigated the effects by maintaining plenty of spare transponder capacity and a 10 percent power margin at the time of their satellite's launch. Under less optimistic assumptions, the losses would approach $70 billion, which is comparable to a year's worth of revenue for all communications satellites. Even this figure does not include the collateral economic losses to the customers of the satellites.

Satellites have been specifically designed to function under the vagaries of space weather. Power grids, in contrast, are fragile at the best of times.

Fortunately, geosynchronous communications satellites are remarkably robust against once-a-decade events, and their life spans have grown from barely five years in 1980 to nearly 17 years today. For solar panels, engineers have switched from silicon to gallium arsenide to increase power production and reduce mass. This move has also provided increased resistance to cosmic-ray damage. Moreover, satellite operators receive advanced storm warnings from the National Oceanic and Atmospheric Administration's Space Weather Prediction Center, which allows them to avoid complex satellite maneuvers or other changes during the time when a storm may arrive. These strategies would doubtless soften the blow of a major storm. To further harden satellites, engineers could thicken the shielding, lower the solar panel voltages to lessen the risk of runaway electrostatic discharges, add extra backup systems and make the software more robust to data corruption.

It is harder to guard against other superstorm effects. X-ray energy deposition would cause the atmosphere to expand, enhancing the drag forces on military and commercial imaging and communications satellites that orbit below 600 kilometers in altitude. Japan's Advanced Satellite for Cosmology and Astrophysics experienced just such conditions during the infamous Bastille Day storm on July 14, 2000, which set in motion a sequence of altitude and power losses that ultimately led to its premature reentry a few months later. During a superstorm, low-orbiting satellites would be at considerable risk of burning up in the atmosphere within weeks or months of the event.

Lights Out

At least our satellites have been specifically designed to function under the vagaries of space weather. Power grids, in contrast, are fragile at the best of times. Every year, according to estimates by Kristina Hamachi-LaCommare and Joseph H. Eto, both at Lawrence Berkeley National Laboratory, the U.S. economy takes an $80-billion hit from localized blackouts and brownouts. Declining power margins over the past decade have also left less excess capacity to keep up with soaring demands.

During solar storms, entirely new problems arise. Large transformers are electrically grounded to Earth and thus susceptible to damage caused by geomagnetically induced direct current (DC). The DC flows up the transformer ground wires and can lead to temperature spikes of 200 degrees Celsius or higher in the transformer windings, causing coolant to vaporize and literally frying the transformer. Even if transformers avoid this fate, the induced current can cause their magnetic cores to saturate during one half of the alternating-current power cycle, distorting the 50- or 60-hertz waveforms. Some of the power is diverted to frequencies that electrical equipment cannot filter out. Instead of humming at a pure pitch, transformers would begin to chatter and screech. Because a magnetic storm affects transformers all over the country, the condition can rapidly escalate to a network-wide collapse of voltage regulation. Grids operate so close to the margin of failure that it would not take much to push them over.

According to studies by John G. Kappenman of Metatech Corporation, the magnetic storm of May 15, 1921, would have caused a blackout affecting half of North America had it happened today. A much larger storm, like that of 1859, could bring down the entire grid. Other industrial countries are also vulnerable, but North America faces greater danger because of its proximity to the north magnetic pole. Because of the physical damage to transformers, full recovery and replacement of damaged components might take weeks or even months. Kappenman testified to Congress in 2003 that "the ability to provide meaningful emergency aid and response to an impacted population that may be in excess of 100 million people will be a difficult challenge."

Ironically, society's increasing vulnerability to solar storms has coincided with decreasing public awareness.

A superstorm will also interfere with radio signals, including those of the Global Positioning System (GPS) and related systems. Intense solar flares not only disturb the ionosphere, through which timing signals propagate, but also produce increased radio noise at GPS frequencies. The result would be position errors of 50 meters or more, rendering GPS useless for many military and civilian applications. A similar loss of precision occurred during the October 29, 2003, storm, which shut down the Wide Area Augmentation System, a radio network that improves the accuracy of GPS position estimates. Commercial aircraft had to resort to in-flight backup systems.

High-energy particles will interfere with aircraft radio communications, especially at high latitudes. United Airlines routinely monitors space weather conditions and has on several occasions diverted polar flights to lower altitudes and latitudes to escape radio interference. A superstorm might force the rerouting of hundreds of flights not just over the pole but also across Canada and the northern U.S. These adverse conditions might last a week.

Getting Ready

Ironically, society's increasing vulnerability to solar storms has coincided with decreasing public awareness. We recently surveyed newspaper coverage of space weather events since the 1840s and discovered that a significant change occurred around 1950. Before this time, magnetic storms, solar flares and their effects often received lavish, front-page stories in newspapers. The *Boston Globe* carried a two-inch headline "U.S. Hit by Magnetic Storm" on March 24, 1940. Since 1950, though, such stories have been buried on inside pages.

Even fairly minor storms are costly. In 2004 Kevin Forbes of the Catholic University of America and Orville Chris St. Cyr of the NASA Goddard Space Flight Center examined the electrical power market from June 1, 2000, to December 31, 2001, and concluded that solar storms increased the wholesale price of electricity during this period by approximately $500 million. Meanwhile the U.S. Department of Defense has estimated that solar disruptions to government satellites cost about $100 million a year. Furthermore, satellite insurers paid out nearly $2 billion between 1996 and 2005 to cover commercial satellite damages and losses, some of which were precipitated by adverse space weather.

Scientists have a long way to go to understand the physics of solar storms and to forecast their effects.

We would be well served by more reliable warnings of solar and geomagnetic storms. With adequate warning, satellite operators can defer critical maneuvering and watch for anomalies that, without quick action, could escalate into critical emergencies. Airline pilots could prepare for an orderly schedule of flight diversions. Power grid operators could watch susceptible network components and make plans to minimize the time the grid might be out of commission.

Agencies such as NASA and the National Science Foundation have worked over the past 20 years to develop space-weather forecasting capabilities. Currently NOAA's Space Weather Prediction Center provides daily space weather reports to more than 1,000 businesses and government agencies. Its annual budget of $6 million is far less than the nearly $500 billion in revenues generated by the industries supported by these forecasts. But this capability relies on a hodgepodge of satellites designed more for research purposes than for efficient, long-term space weather monitoring.

Some researchers feel our ability to predict space weather is about where NOAA was in predicting atmospheric weather in the early 1950s. From a monitoring perspective, what are needed are inexpensive, long-term space buoys to monitor weather conditions using simple, off-the-shelf instruments. In the meantime, scientists have a long way to go to understand the physics of solar storms and to forecast their effects. If we really want to safeguard our technological infrastructure, we will have to redouble our investment in forecasting, modeling and basic research to batten down for the next solar tempest.

8

The World Needs a Global Warning System for Solar Storms

Dan Reynolds

Dan Reynolds is the senior editor of Risk & Insurance, *a trade magazine for the insurance industry.*

In June 2011, the sun hurled a coronal mass ejection (CME) toward Earth during a solar storm. The photos from space depicted a powerful and awe-inspiring explosion, but most people did not even know it happened because it did not cause any damage. But the only reason that there were not devastating consequences for our modern technological infrastructure is that the energy from the CME did not hit the Earth's magnetic field in a disruptive way. It was little more than a glancing blow because of the way the Earth's magnetic field and that of the sun were aligned. But if such a CME were to hit the Earth's magnetic field directly, it would be catastrophic. It could very well happen, and that is why scientists want to bolster the International Space Environment Service's global space weather and data sharing centers. The hope is to be able to predict the magnetic field direction of an incoming CME so that the severity of such an event could be anticipated and prepared for.

The images, when they were posted on the web, were awe-inspiring and a little bit frightening.

On June 7 [2011] a coronal mass ejection, a massive energy eruption on the surface of the sun, sent cosmic energy flying through space and toward Earth.

Because of our advanced space photography, we could see the explosion in great detail. The image resembled what it would look like if someone had thrown a rock into a pond filled with red water, and the reactive energy was high and spread out.

The energy from coronal mass ejections takes an average of three days to reach us, and this CME struck our magnetic field at around 1 p.m. EST on June 10, [2011] said Mike Hapgood, head of the Space Environment Group at RAL Space, in Oxford, England.

The good news is that almost nothing happened.

More of these [coronal mass] ejections are likely on the way, and we might not be so lucky the next time.

"I think it's a wonderful event. It is spectacular in the imagery, but I think there is a kind of an element of: A) it largely missed and B) when it got here, it was ineffective," said Hapgood, a visiting professor at Lancaster University and an international authority on space weather.

There are reasons for that. One, when the solar mass left the sun, it was ejected from a part of the sun with a northward-facing magnetic field. The side of earth facing the sun also has a northerly directed field. So, when the coronal mass ejection struck our magnetic field on June 10, the two northern facing fields just bounced off one another.

Secondly, the coronal mass ejection struck us at an oblique angle, bouncing off of our magnetic field and doing little damage.

When Luck Runs Out

But all of that could change as simply as you flip a coin.

One, we are just in the beginning stages of the most recent 11-year solar weather cycle, which began in January of 2008. More of these ejections are likely on the way, and we might not be so lucky the next time.

If a coronal mass ejection were to leave the sun with a southern-facing magnetic field and strike us more directly, it would temporarily unpeel the Earth's magnetic field. That's a phenomenon scientists call magnetic reconnection, when the Earth's magnetic field breaks apart and reforms.

As fantastic as that sounds, it has happened before. The most impactful coronal mass ejection in recorded memory was the Carrington Event, so named for the English vicar who recorded it in 1859. Back in Carrington's day, the coronal mass ejection fried telegraph wires in the United Kingdom and the United States. In our modern world, with grids of electronic transformers, satellite networks, and financial and communications systems that depend on electronic trading and transmission, the results could well be catastrophic.

The worst modern occurrence of a CME knocked out power for some residents of Quebec for as long as six days in 1989. Longer blackouts over a wider area are possible and could wreak all kinds of havoc, according to Lloyd's [of London Insurance] and sources with other major carriers.

Strengthening the Global Alert System

That's why Hapgood and others are pushing to strengthen our global alert network for solar storms. The International Space Environment Service has established 13 global space weather warning and data sharing centers around the world.

Hapgood and other scientists are also trying to advance their knowledge of the nature of coronal mass ejections to be able to forecast whether they have south-facing magnetic fields, and thus warn operators of satellites and commercial and scientific users that depend on the space weather warning service.

"It is a research goal to be able to predict the magnetic field direction at Earth given what we know of conditions on the sun," Hapgood said.

"The northerly and southerly fields occur in equal proportions, but what we see today appears random because we can't yet do the physics well. But a lot of folks are now working on this," Hapgood said.

9

NASA Hopes New "Solar Shield" Will Predict Storm Severity

Nola Redd

Nola Redd is a freelance journalist who writes about space and science for media outlets such as Scientific American *and* CBS News. *She is a regular contributor to* Space.com, *and she writes an astrophysics blog for the American Museum of Natural History.*

The National Aeronautics and Space Administration (NASA) has launched a new project, called "Solar Shield," in the hopes of someday being able to reliably predict space weather events. The main focus of Solar Shield is studying the massive sun eruptions called mass coronal ejections (CMEs), which are hurled toward Earth during a solar storm. It is these CMEs that disrupt the Earth's magnetic field and can cripple power grids and the high-tech infrastructure. If the severity of a CME can be reliably predicted ahead of time, it might be possible to take steps to prevent the worst types of damage. The Solar Shield project is in its beginning stages, and the science of space-weather prediction itself is in its infancy. NASA hopes that more companies will help improve Solar Shield by supplying data that it can use in its research.

NASA has devised a new tool in the battle against massive eruptions from the sun: an early warning system to protect electrical grids on Earth from extremely powerful solar storms.

The new project, called Solar Shield, is designed to predict the severity of powerful sun storms at specific locations on Earth to help power companies plan responses and limit the potential damage to their equipment.

"It amounts to knowing 'something is coming and it may be big,'" project leader Antti Pulkkinen, a research associate at NASA's Goddard Space Flight Center in Greenbelt, Md., told SPACE.com. But Solar Shield should provide "much more specificity."

The predictions from NASA's Solar Shield could potentially help avoid the worst of the damage.

Massive Sun Eruptions

The chief targets for NASA's Solar Shield are huge sun eruptions called coronal mass ejections, or CMEs, which can shoot off billions of tons of plasma and charged particles.

The sun is currently going through a more active phase of its 11-year solar weather cycle. It has been emerging from a prolonged lull in activity and is expected to hit the peak of the current cycle in 2013.

When the magnetic field associated with a CME encounters the Earth's magnetic field, the two merge and an enormous amount of energy is transferred to the geomagnetosphere. This resulting current can affect astronauts or satellites in space, as well as commercial power grids.

If the CME is strong enough, the grids can become overburdened or damaged. The resulting blackout could last anywhere from hours to months, depending on the amount of damage sustained.

Strong CMEs are classified as low-frequency/high-impact events, meaning that while they are rare, their consequences are far-reaching, researchers said.

A 2008 workshop by the National Research Council's Space Studies Board predicted that a "severe geomagnetic storm scenario" would have societal and economic costs of up to $2 trillion in the first year alone, and recovery time ranging from four to 10 years.

The predictions from NASA's Solar Shield could potentially help avoid the worst of the damage, researchers said.

Calculating Risk

The project aims to minimize the effects by providing both short- and long-term predictions regarding impending CMEs. Today, scientists can tell when an ejection is headed towards Earth, but the data is very generalized.

Different power nodes are affected by the resulting magnetic storms in different ways. Part of this depends on the time of day; systems are more vulnerable during non-peak usage hours.

Location also factors in. High latitude locations experience more dramatic impacts than their low latitude counterparts. Another factor is local geology; the resulting currents are affected by the ground conductivity.

So each node faces a different level of risk, which Solar Shield aims to calculate. But how do they do it?

It goes something like this: Once a coronal mass ejection is registered, data from the sun-watching observatories like the SOHO spacecraft and NASA's twin Stereo satellites allow the team to create a 3-D model and provide a relatively long-term prediction as to its arrival time, ranging anywhere from 24 to 48 hours.

While the CME travels through space, the team uses the computers at Goddard's Community Coordinated Modeling Center (CCMC) to create generalized predictions. As the stream of particles moves closer to Earth, it passes NASA's Advanced Composition Explorer—a space weather monitoring satellite—about 30 to 60 minutes before reaching our planet.

The ACE satellite collects real-time data, enabling the team to quickly refine and narrow their predictions. NASA then notifies the Electric Power Research Institute's Sunburst program with their results.

"We quickly feed the data into CCMC computers," Pulkkinen explained in a statement. "Our models predict fields and currents in Earth's upper atmosphere and propagate these currents down to the ground."

More real-life observations and partners among the power industry are needed to refine the processes.

Still Under Development

Pulkkinen said the Solar Shield project is still in the experimental stage and more data—meaning more solar activity observations—will be needed to refine it. But he hopes that more individual power companies will be able to turn to the EPRI to receive both forecasts and real-time information for the approaching storm.

Each node could then take the action it deems appropriate, based on localized predictions. These actions could include simple things such as canceling planned maintenance work or having more employees on hand to deal with resulting surges, or stronger tactics like disconnecting the most vulnerable transformers from the grid itself. Such a controlled power outage only would be temporary, and far less damaging than an externally induced blackout.

However, a false alarm could be costly to the electric companies, so more real-life observations and partners among the power industry are needed to refine the processes, Pulkkinen said.

"We'd like more power companies to join our research effort," he added. "The more data we can collect from the field, the faster we can test and improve Solar Shield."

10

Solar Storms Make Airplane Travel More Dangerous

Patrick Lynch

Patrick Lynch is a writer with the Science Mission Directorate at the National Aeronautics and Space Administration (NASA) Langley Research Center.

For the first time, a National Aeronautics and Space Administration (NASA) study about radiation exposure for airline pilots and passengers includes the radiation emitted by solar storms. NASA reports that not considering solar storm data in past research could have lead to underestimating radiation exposure during flight by up to 300 percent. The recent findings show that radiation exposure is significantly higher on international flights, which fly at higher altitudes where radiation from solar storms is present. Cancer risk increases along with radiation exposure, and it is of particular concern for pilots and flight crew who are exposed on a regular basis throughout their careers. Learning more about how and when planes encounter radiation during flight could eventually lead to routine in-flight radiation monitoring and to pilots adjusting flight plans according to radiation risk, like they do for inclement weather.

Scientists at NASA's [National Aeronautics and Space Administration] Langley Research Center have completed a first attempt to accurately calculate the level of damaging radiation flight crews and passengers are exposed to on com-

Patrick Lynch, "Solar Storms and Radiation Exposure on Commercial Flights," NASA. gov, December 15, 2009.

mercial airline flights. The work is an early step toward developing a model to observe radiation exposure for all commercial flights, particularly for pilots and crews who spend their careers airborne and who are at greater risk of developing certain cancers.

The study considered not only everyday radiation emanating from space, but also the additional energy unleashed during a solar storm, which can be profound. NASA scientists say not including geomagnetic effects on solar radiation in modeling radiation exposure could underestimate the dosage by 30 to 300 percent.

Researchers looked at passengers and crew on typical flights from Chicago to Beijing, Chicago to Stockholm and London to New York, during what is known as the Halloween 2003 Storm. These flights were chosen because of their long flight paths near the North Pole, where the Earth's natural protection from radiation is weakest. Earth's magnetic field approaches zero above the poles. The Halloween 2003 event was chosen because it was both a large and a complex storm, making it a good test for the model.

Violent storms on the [sun's] surface eject powerful bursts of radiation to the Earth. It is these events that have never been truly accounted for in studies of how much radiation pilots and airline passengers are exposed to.

The Study Results

The study found that aircrew and passengers during the Chicago to Beijing flight, for example, would have been exposed to about 12 percent of the annual radiation limit recommended by the International Committee on Radiological Protection. But these exposures were greater than on typical flights at lower latitudes, and confirmed the concerns about commercial flights at high latitudes.

"The upshot is that these international flights were right there at that boundary where many of these events can take place, where radiation exposure can be much higher," said Chris Mertens, senior research scientist at NASA's Langley Research Center, who is leading the research effort. Mertens will present his latest results at the American Geophysical Union fall meeting in San Francisco on Dec. 16 [2009].

Piecing together the radiation exposure on these typical flights is the first step toward developing a real-time system that researchers hope will become a standard component of commercial airline cockpits. Radiation exposure could one day be taken into account in the same way weather conditions are considered before deciding to fly or deciding what exact route to fly and at what altitude.

The number of international flights that skirt the north pole are increasing. Airlines save massive amounts of fuel on flights such as Chicago-to-Shanghai by simply flying "over the top"—it is a far shorter route than following the latitude lines. But while saving fuel, these flight paths take planes and their passengers to the thinner layers of Earth's magnetosphere, which shields potentially harmful solar and cosmic radiation.

On a typical day, the Sun is quiet and "background radiation," the cumulative effect of radiation from cosmic sources reaching Earth, is the only other source. But when the Sun is not quiet, violent storms on the star's surface eject powerful bursts of radiation to the Earth. It is these events that have never been truly accounted for in studies of how much radiation pilots and airline passengers are exposed to.

Studies . . . show pilots face a four-times greater risk of melanoma than the general population.

Pilots Are Not Monitored for Radiation

While the flights studied appear to have not put passengers in danger of exceeding the safe radiation limit in an individual flight, concerns remain, Mertens said. Many workers whose jobs expose them to consistent radiation sources log that exposure to keep a record over one's career. People who work on commercial airline flights are technically listed as "radiation workers" by the federal government—a classification that includes nuclear plant workers and X-ray technicians. But unlike some others in that category, flight crews do not quantify the radiation they are exposed to.

Mike Holland, an American Airlines captain and vice chairman for radiation and environmental issues with the Allied Pilots Association, said he is following Mertens' research with interest. The pilots association has written a formal letter in support of the research. Holland cited studies that show pilots face a four-times greater risk of melanoma than the general population. But because pilots and flight crews do not wear radiation-measuring badges like other radiation workers, the only estimates about their career-long exposure come from models.

Hoping for Answers

Up until now, most of those models only attempted to capture the amount of cosmic background radiation that reaches airliners in flight. Holland said he believes including solar radiation, especially during solar storms, is important. He looks forward to having answers for the pilots who contact him with questions about radiation and cancer risk.

"When I talk to epidemiologists, they have two questions for me: What is your exposure? And what is your health for 20 to 30 years after you retire?" Holland said. The second question he and other pilots can answer, in time. But as of now, they can't measure their exposure.

"We're excited that Chris is doing this," Holland said, "and we hope it can answer the epidemiologists first question, which is, 'What is your exposure?'"

11

Solar Storms Do Not Cause Global Warming

Brian Handwerk

Brian Handwerk is a science writer whose work regularly appears in National Geographic News *online.*

Scientists as far back as Galileo have tried to understand the link between the sun and the Earth's climate, and modern researchers still debate the sun's influence. A recent report, however, concludes that sunspot-driven changes in the sun's overall power output—such as solar storms—affect the amount of energy the Earth gets from the sun but not enough to have an impact on global climate change. Solar astronomer Peter Foukal analyzed historical solar data observed from the seventeenth to the twenty-first century and found that the difference in power between the high point of a sunspot cycle (the solar maximum when solar storms typically occur) and its low point is less than 0.1 percent of the sun's total output. Foukal concluded that the difference is not big enough to have a significant impact on planetary climate change. Other experts point out that there could still be other unknown solar mechanisms that affect the Earth's climate.

Sunspots alter the amount of energy Earth gets from the sun, but not enough to impact global climate change, a new study suggests.

The sun's role in global warming has long been a matter of debate and is likely to remain a contentious topic.

Solar astronomer Peter Foukal of Heliophysics, Inc., in Nahant, Massachusetts, points out that scientists have pondered the link between the sun and Earth's climate since the time of Galileo, the famous 17th-century astronomer.

"There has been an intuitive perception that the sun's variable degree of brightness—the coming and going of sunspots for instance—might have an impact on climate," Foukal said.

Foukal is lead author of a review paper on sunspot intensity appearing in [the Sept. 14, 2006] issue of the journal *Nature*.

He says that most climate models—including ones used by the Intergovernmental Panel on Climate Change—already incorporate the effects of the sun's waxing and waning power on Earth's weather.

But, Foukal said, "this paper says that that particular mechanism [sunspots], which is most intuitive, is probably not having an impact."

The sun's energy output varies slightly as sunspots wax and wane on the star's surface.

Sunspot Impact Simply Too Small

Sunspots are magnetic disturbances that appear as cooler, dark patches on the sun's surface. The number of spots cycles over time, reaching a peak every 11 years.

The spots' impact on the sun's total energy output is easy to see.

"As it turns out, most of the sun's power output is in the visible range—what we see as brightness," said Henk Spruit, study co-author from the Max Planck Institute for Astrophysics in Garching, Germany.

"The sun's brightness varies only because of the blemishes that are also visible directly on pictures: the dark patches called sunspots and the minute bright points called faculae. In terms of brightness changes, in large part, what you see is what you get."

The sun's energy output varies slightly as sunspots wax and wane on the star's surface.

But sunspot-driven changes to the sun's power are simply too small to account for the climatic changes observed in historical data from the 17th century to the present, research suggests.

The difference in brightness between the high point of a sunspot cycle and its low point is less than 0.1 percent of the sun's total output.

"If you run that back in time to the 17th century using sunspot records, you'll find that this amplitude variance is negligible for climate," Foukal said.

Measuring Historical Data

The researchers obtained accurate daily sunspot measurements dating as far back as 1874 from institutions such as the Mount Wilson Observatory near Pasadena, California, and the Royal Observatory in Greenwich, England.

Older records exist all the way back to when the telescope was invented in the 17th century, though the data become increasingly patchy with age.

The team also derived the sun's historic strength by looking at the presence or absence of isotopes, such as beryllium 10, in ice samples from Greenland and Antarctic that reflect the past contents of Earth's atmosphere.

Such isotopes are formed when cosmic radiation penetrates the atmosphere.

In periods of high activity, a brighter sun emits more magnetic and plasmatic particles that shield Earth from the galaxy's rays, resulting in fewer isotopes.

Measuring the historical record of such isotopes from ice yields useful, though debatable, estimates of the sun's past power on Earth.

"If you see that these isotopes were low for 50 or 100 years, it's a damn good bet that the sun was more active then," Foukal said.

The authors and other experts are quick to point out that more complicated solar mechanisms could possibly be driving climate change in ways we don't yet understand.

Climate change carries such high stakes that even more unlikely possibilities may capture scientific attention.

Other Sun Events May Be Factors

"There are numerous studies that find a correlation [between solar variation and Earth climate]," said Sami Solanki of the Max Planck Institute for Solar System Research in Lindau, Germany.

"These authors have looked at the simplest mechanism, and they find that this mechanism does not produce the same level of change that has been observed," he continued.

"This could be suggesting that there are other mechanisms acting for the way that the sun influences climate."

Solar ultraviolet (UV) rays are one possibility, though that theory creates its own challenges.

"UV is only a small fraction of total solar output, so you'd need a strong amplification mechanism in the Earth's atmosphere," study co-author Spruit said.

Magnetized plasma flares known as solar wind could also impact Earth's climate. Solar wind influences galactic rays and may in turn affect atmospheric phenomena on Earth, such as cloud cover.

Such complex interactions are poorly understood but could be crucial to unlocking Earth's climatic puzzle.

"I think the main question," the Max Planck Institute's Solanki said, "is, How does the sun [in general] act on climate? What are the processes that are going on in the Earth's atmosphere?"

Organizations to Contact

The editors have compiled the following list of organizations concerned with the issues debated in this book. The descriptions are derived from materials provided by the organizations. All have publications or information available for interested readers. The list was compiled on the date of publication of the present volume; the information provided here may change. Be aware that many organizations take several weeks or longer to respond to inquiries, so allow as much time as possible.

Astronomical League
9201 Ward Parkway, Suite 100, Kansas City, MO   64114
(816) 333-7759
e-mail: leagueoffice@astroleague.org
website: www.astroleague.org

The Astronomical League is the umbrella organization of more than two hundred and forty amateur astronomy organizations across the United States. The League's mission is to promote the science of astronomy through encouraging public interest and participation in local astronomy clubs. The Astronomical League publishes a monthly newsletter and the quarterly magazine, *The Reflector*, and it provides a variety of "observing" awards to members for locating and describing certain specified astronomical objects or events. The Astronomical League website includes listings for amateur astronomy clubs and events nationwide, details about its National Observing Program, daily news updates and videos, and extensive links to other organizations relevant to those who have an interest in space, astronomy, stargazing, and weather phenomena.

European Space Agency (ESA)
955 L'Enfant Plaza SW, Suite 7800, Washington, DC   20024
(202) 488-4158 • fax: (202) 488-4930
website: www.esa.int

Headquartered in Paris, the European Space Agency (ESA) is a collective of eighteen member nations that work together to fund various space projects. The organization promotes space exploration and members share the costs of manned and un-manned missions into space. The ESA website features a daily photo log, called "The Sun Now," which depicts the sun as seen from the Solar and Heliospheric Observatory (SOHO), stationed 1.5 million kilometers from Earth. SOHO constantly watches the Sun and returns data and spectacular color pictures of spots, flares, storms, and other phenomena that rage across the star's surface. The SOHO mission is a joint ESA/National Aeronautics and Space Administration (NASA) project. Experts around the world use SOHO images and data to help them predict space weather events.

Federal Aviation Administration (FAA)
800 Independence Ave. SW, Washington, DC   20591
(866) 835-5322
website: www.faa.gov

The Federal Aviation Administration is the government agency that is responsible for regulating air travel in the United States. As commercial space travel and tourism becomes a reality, it is also the agency that will be charged with ensuring the safe operation of this burgeoning industry. The FAA website includes information about solar storms as the topic pertains to airline and commercial space travel. Documents available on the site include the FAA's various regulations, policies, and advisories to pilots, as well as the report "Ionizing Radiation in Earth's Atmosphere and in Space Near Earth," and the general space primer "Space In Our Lives."

Lunar and Planetary Institute (LPI)
3600 Bay Area Blvd., Houston, TX   77058
(281) 486-2100
e-mail: webmaster@lpi.usra.edu
website: www.lpi.usra.edu

LPI was founded in 1968 to be a central research agency that facilitates cooperation between scientists to enhance human understanding of the universe. The three main areas on which the institute focuses are research science, service to the National Aeronautics and Space Administration (NASA) and the planetary science community, and education and public outreach. Through these efforts, LPI seeks to foster communication between scientists and the public and encourage excitement about space research and exploration. The organization's website provides resources such as planetary journals, maps, and images. Sun-specific content includes the e-book, *About Our Sun*, sun-themed "Sky Teller" youth activities, and the report titled "Solar History Effects on Venus and Earth Climate."

National Aeronautics and Space Administration (NASA)

300 E St. SW, Suite 5K39, Washington, DC   20546-0001
(202) 358-0001 • fax: (202) 358-4338
website: www.nasa.gov

The National Aeronautics and Space Administration (NASA) is the US government agency responsible for the nation's civilian space program as well as aeronautics and aerospace research. The NASA website features information about all of NASA's many projects, as well as space and astronomy topics in general. The site offers extensive information about the sun and solar storms, including stunning videos of the X1.8 class flare and coronal mass ejection that occurred January 27, 2012. Other resources include the articles "Killer Solar Flares Are a Physical Impossibility" and "2012: Beginning of the End or Why the World Won't End," which explains NASA's position about 2012–13 solar storm predictions.

National Space Society (NSS)

1155 15th St. NW, Suite 500, Washington, DC   20005
(202) 429-1600 • fax: (202) 530-0659
e-mail: nsshq@nss.org
website: www.nss.org

As a grassroots, nonprofit organization, the National Space Society (NSS) works to promote space travel and the expansion of human civilization beyond Earth. The Society maintains that space exploration and colonization is necessary to ensure the survival of the human race in the face of increasing threats on Earth. Information about space travel, space settlements, space tourism, the sun, and other topics can be found on the NSS website and in the organization's quarterly journal, *Ad Astra*. The organization's site includes such resources as a "Solar Storms Information Sheet" and an interactive solar storm plotting graph that demonstrates the relationship between sun phenomena and effects on Earth.

National Space Weather Program (NSWP)
e-mail: michael.bonadonna@noaa.gov
website: www.nswp.gov/

The National Space Weather Program (NSWP) is an interagency program whose mission is to improve space weather observation and forecasting. It emerged in 1994 from the efforts of several US government agencies to prepare the country to deal with technological vulnerabilities associated with the space environment. The overarching goal of the NSWP is to create a system where agencies—such as NASA, the Space Weather Prediction Center, and the Air Force—can work together to provide timely, accurate, and reliable space weather warnings, observations, and forecasts. The NSWP website features information about all of its programs as well as numerous documents and reports about solar storms.

SETI Institute
189 Bernardo Ave., Suite 100, Mountain View, CA   94043
(650) 961-6633 • fax: (650) 961-7099
e-mail: info@seti.org
website: www.seti.org

SETI Institute is a private nonprofit organization founded with the goal of researching, discovering, and explaining the origin, nature, and prevalence of life in the universe. Since its founding in 1984, SETI scientists have worked to achieve this goal in coordination with NASA and other private space exploration and science organizations. One of the major branches of the organization is the Carl Sagan Center for the Study of Life in the Universe, which is an umbrella group for other projects such as "The Formation and Evolution of Planetary Systems: Placing Our Solar System in Context" and "From Habitability to Life." The SETI website features information about all of its projects as well as education and outreach materials. One article of interest may be "The Future of Forecasting Earthquakes," which discusses the possible relationship between solar flares and earthquakes.

Space Studies Board

500 Fifth St. NW, Washington, DC   20001
(202) 334-3477 • fax: (202) 334-3701
e-mail: ssb@nas.edu
website: http://sites.nationalacademies.org/SSB/

The Committee on the Societal and Economic Impacts of Severe Space Weather Events is a committee of the Space Studies Board of the National Research Council (NRC), a nonprofit organization that conducts research for and provides expert advice to Congress and federal agencies. In 2008, the Committee conducted extensive research and held numerous workshops to investigate the potential impact of a severe solar storm on the Earth. Its report, *Severe Space Weather Events: Understanding Societal and Economic Impacts: A Workshop Report*, is available in its entirety as a PDF from the Space Studies Board section of the NRC website.

Space Weather Prediction Center (SWPC)

National Oceanic and Atmospheric Administration (NOAA)
1401 Constitution Ave. NW, Room 5128
Washington, DC   20230
(301) 713-1208
e-mail: outreach@noaa.gov
website: www.swpc.noaa.gov

The National Oceanic and Atmospheric Administration (NOAA, pronounced "noah") is a scientific agency within the US Department of Commerce that focuses on the conditions of the oceans and the atmosphere. The NOAA Space Weather Prediction Center (SWPC) is the nation's official source of space weather alerts, watches, and warnings. The SWPC provides real-time monitoring and forecasting of solar and geophysical events that impact satellites, power grids, communications, navigation, and other technological systems. The SWPC also explores and evaluates new models and products and transitions them into operations. NOAA's SWPC website offers a wide variety of alerts, timelines, reports, and summaries about solar storms and other space weather events.

Universe Today
e-mail: info@universetoday.com
website: www.universetoday.com

Universe Today is a non-commercial space and astronomy news and community web forum that has been online since 1999. Featuring daily astronomy news stories, commentaries, photos, and videos, the website also offers a Guide to Space, an extensive collection of space-related fact sheets on topics ranging from planets in this solar system, to outer space, to astronomy equipment reviews. The Guide to Space section for the Sun covers scores of sun-related topics, including solar storms and solar maximums and minimums, and it provides answers to questions such as "will the sun explode?," "how hot is the surface of the sun?," and "why are sunsets red?" The website is well regarded and attracts several million visitors per year, many of whom are professional astrophysicists and astronomers who participate in the online discussions.

Bibliography

Books

Pål Brekke	*Our Explosive Sun: A Visual Feast of Our Source of Light and Life.* New York: Springer, 2011.
John Eddy	*The Sun, the Earth, and Near-Earth Space: A Guide to the Sun-Earth System.* National Aeronautics and Space Administration (NASA). Washington, DC: US Government Printing Office, 2009.
Ron Foster	*The Season of the Solar Storm: Christmas Dreams and a Preppers Nightmare.* Seattle: CreateSpace, 2011.
Ron Foster and Cheryl Chamlies	*Our End of the Lake: Surviving After the 2012 Solar Storm.* Seattle: CreateSpace, 2011.
John Freeman	*Storms in Space.* Boston: Cambridge University Press, 2001.
Hannu Koskinen	*Physics of Space Storms: From the Solar Surface to the Earth.* New York: Springer Praxis Books/Environmental Sciences, 2011.
James Marusek	*Solar Storm Threat Analysis.* Bloomfield, IN: Impact, 2007.
Richard Muller	*Physics for Future Presidents.* Des Moines, IA: National Geographic Books, 2007.

Sten F. Odenwald   *The Astronomy Cafe.* San Francisco: W.H. Freeman, 1998.

Sten F. Odenwald   *The 23rd Cycle: Learning to Live with a Stormy Star.* New York: Columbia University Press, 2001. Out of print but available as a PDF at www.solarstorms.org/S23rdCycle.html.

Larry Poole   *EMP Survival: How to Prepare Now and Survive, When an Electromagnetic Pulse Destroys Our Power Grid.* Seattle: CreateSpace, 2011.

Barbara Poppe and Kristen Jorden   *Sentinels of the Sun: Forecasting Space Weather.* Boulder, CO: Johnson Books, 2006.

Steven Suess and Bruce Tsurutani   *From the Sun: Auroras, Magnetic Storms, Solar Flares, Cosmic Rays.* Washington, DC: American Geophysical Union, 1998.

Periodicals and Internet Sources

Benjamin Anastas   "The Final Days," *New York Times Magazine*, July 1, 2007.

Kurt Andersen   "The End of the World As They Know It," *New York Magazine*, February 26, 2006.

Simon Atkins   "Powerful Solar Storm Could Shut Down USA for Months: Oh Please, Enough Drama," *G+*, June 17, 2010. www.gplus.com.

Mitch Battros   "Solar Activity Affects Humans'
                       Physical and Mental State,"
                       Sunlightenment, December 12, 2008.
                       http://sunlightenment.com.

Peter Behr   "This Week's Solar Flare Illuminates
                       the Grid's Vulnerability," *New York
                       Times*, June 9, 2011.

James Borges   "Sunspots and Human Behavior,"
                       Journal of Borderland Research, Vol.
                       56, No. 1, 2000.

Steve Connor   "Relax, the End Isn't Nigh," *The
                       Independent (UK)*, October 17, 2009.

Michael Crowley   "The Newt Bomb: How a
                       Pulp-Fiction Fantasy Became a GOP
                       Weapons Craze," *The New Republic*,
                       June 3, 2009.

Clay Dillow   "NASA Is Building a 'Solar Shield' to
                       Protect Power Grids from Space
                       Weather," *Popsci*, October 28, 2010.
                       www.popsci.com.

Charmaine   "The Effect of Geomagnetic Storms
Gordon and   on Suicide," *South African Psychiatry
Michael Berk   Review*, No. 6, 2003.

Jon Hamilton   "Solar Storms Could Be Earth's Next
                       Katrina," *NPR*, February 26, 2010.
                       www.npr.org.

Michael Hesse et al.   "Benchmark Report for Integrated Forecasting System for Mitigating Adverse Space Weather Effects on the Northern American High-Voltage Power Transmission System," *NASA Applied Sciences Program Report*, January 2009. http://ccmc.gsfc.nasa.gov.

Victoria Jaggard   "Magnetic-Shield Cracks Found; Big Solar Storms Expected," *National Geographic News*, December 17, 2008.

R.W. Kay   "Geomagnetic Storms: Association with Incidence of Depression as Measured by Hospital Admission," *The British Journal of Psychiatry*, No. 164, 1994.

Brian Kennedy   "What a Single Nuclear Warhead Could Do," *Wall Street Journal*, November 24, 2008.

Richard Kerr   "Are We Ready for the Next Solar Maximum? No Way, Say Scientists," *Science*, No. 324, 2009.

Anna Krivelyova and Cesare Robotti   "Playing the Field: Geomagnetic Storms and International Stock Markets," Federal Reserve Bank of Atlanta, February 2003. www.frbatlanta.org.

V.P. Kuleshova et al.   "Biotropic Effects of Geomagnetic Storms and Their Seasonal Variations," *Biofizika*, Vol. 46, No. 5, September–October 2001.

Stew Magnuson and Dan Parsons — "Solar Storms Could Plunge Nation into Darkness," *National Defense*, November 22, 2011.

Kennedy Maize — "The Great Solar Storm of 2012?" *Power*, January 2, 2011.

Jena Baker McNeill and Richard Weitz — "Electromagnetic Pulse (EMP) Attack: A Preventable Homeland Security Catastrophe," The Heritage Foundation, October 20, 2008. www.heritage.org.

Anne Minard — "Sun's Power Hits New Low, May Endanger Earth?" *National Geographic News*, September 24, 2008.

National Oceanic and Atmospheric Administration (NOAA) — "Space Weather Primer," NOAA Space Weather Prediction Center, 2006. www.swpc.noaa.gov.

Deborah Netburn — "Solar Storms May Cause Cellphones to Drop Calls," *Los Angeles Times*, January 24, 2012.

Rosalba O'Brien — "Riots, Wild Markets: Did Space Storms Drive Us Mad?" *Reuters*, August 12, 2011.

Sid Perkins — "Potential Predictor of Solar Storms: Microwave Bursts May Warn of Impending Eruption from Sun," *Science News*, September 8, 2010.

Tony Phillips — "Deep Solar Minimum," *NASA Science News*, April 1, 2009. http://science.nasa.gov.

Tony Phillips	"The Surprising Shape of Solar Storms," *NASA Science News*, April 14, 2009. http://science.nasa.gov.
Dan Reynolds	"Solar Storms Are Real Risk: A Weakened Power Grid, Higher Demand and Powerful Space Waves Make for a Scary Mix," *Risk and Insurance*, November 5, 2010.
Nick Schwellenbach	"The EMP(ty) Threat?" *Washington Times*, November 27, 2005.
Al Slavin	"Too Much Sun: A New Solar Cycle Refuels Concerns over the Potential Impact of Geomagnetic Storms," *Best's Review*, August 2, 2010.
Curt Suplee	"The Sun: Living with a Stormy Star," *National Geographic*, June 17, 2004.
Steve Tracton	"Do Solar Storms Threaten Life as We Know It?" *Washington Post* "Capitol Weather Gang" blog. April 6, 2009. http://voices.washingtonpost.com.
Steve Tracton	"Space Weather: Are We Ready for a Solar Strike?" *Washington Post* "Capitol Weather Gang" blog, March 9, 2011. http://voices.washingtonpost.com.

Cyril Tuohy   "Solar Storms Are Mere Spin: Solar
                     Storms Are a Phantom Menace Way
                     out of Proportion to the Perceived
                     Threat," *Risk and Insurance*,
                     November 5, 2010.

Index

A

Advanced Composition Explorer (ACE)
    data collection by, 11–12, 19, 72
    measurements by, 25
    reliability of, 50–51
Advanced Satellite for Cosmology and Astrophysics, 60–61
Aerobraking effect, 26
Air travel
    danger to, 74–77
    radiation exposure, 74–76
    radiation monitoring, 76–77
    rerouting, 7, 13–14, 62
Allied Pilots Association, 77
American Association for the Advancement of Science, 9, 31
American Geophysical Union, 76
Anik satellites, 19, 59
Antarctica, 56, 80

B

Back-up generators, 47
Baker, Daniel, 31–33, 44, 52
Bastille Day storm (2000), 60–61
Berra, Yogi, 40–41
Biesecker, Doug, 36
Black-outs, 11, 14–16, 39
Bogdan, Tom, 31–32, 34, 38
Boston Globe (newspaper), 63
Boyle, Alan, 39–42
Brooks, Michael, 43–52

C

C-class flares, 8
Canada, 11, 13, 27, 44
Carrington, Richard, 31, 45, 54
Carrington Event (1859)
    as benchmark, 45–46, 50
    communication failures from, 8
    discovery of, 31, 54–55
    impact of, 31–32, 36–37, 40, 67
    socioeconomic disruptions from, 16
    solar cycle during, 52
Catholic University of America, 63
China, 49
Climate change, 79, 81
Cliver, Ed, 31–33
Committee on the Societal and Economic Impacts of Severe Space Weather Events, 10–20
Communication disturbances
    overview, 30–31
    preparedness over, 41–42
    satellite tests, 59–60
    from solar storms, 7, 30–34
    telecommunication concerns, 13
    See also Global Positioning System (GPS) satellites; Satellites
Communications/Navigation Outage Forecasting System, 17
Community Coordinated Modeling Center (CCMC), 71–72
Cornell University, 48

Coronal mass ejection (CME)
  with Carrington event, 57–58
  defined, 45, 56, 70
  fears of, 26–27
  images of, 65–66
  overview, 25
  predicting, 18–19, 67, 70–71
  solar storm from, 7–8, 32
  speed of, 50
Cyber cocoon, 32–33

D

Defense Meteorological Satellites
  Program, 17
Digital Ionospheric Sounding System, 17
Direct current (DC), 61
Doomsday fears, 22, 39–42, 44

E

Earth-Sun Lagrangian point, 25
Earth's magnetic field. See Magnetosphere
Earth's poles, 7
Electric power. See Power grids
Electric Power Research Institute's
  Sunburst program, 72
Electrojet current, 27, 29
Electromagnetic burst, 7, 32
Energetic protons, 58–59
Eto, Joseph H., 61
Europe, 36–37, 49, 54
European Space Agency, 49

F

Federal Aviation Administration
  (FAA), 13, 14
Fisher, Richard, 40–41

Forbes, Kevin, 63
Foukal, Peter, 79, 80
France, 49
Fuel pipelines, 48

G

Gamma rays, 57
Geomagnetic storms/disturbances
  in Canada, 11
  defense against, 14
  impact of, 19, 40–41, 48–49,
    55
  prediction of, 18, 50, 63, 71
  radiation danger from, 75
  satellite danger from, 59–61
  superstorms, 16, 58
  from X-class flare, 8
  See also Carrington Event;
    Solar storms
Geomagnetically induced currents
  (GICs), 14
Geosynchronous communications
  satellites, 60
Germany, 49, 79, 81
Global Positioning System (GPS)
  satellites
  as forecast systems, 19
  impact on, 13, 17, 29, 32, 62
  modernization of, 14
  navigation signals from, 11
  Wide Area Augmentation System (WAAS), 13
Global warming
  climate change from, 79, 81
  historical data on, 80–81
  other sun events and, 81–82
  overview, 78–79
  from solar storms, 78–82
  sunspot activity and, 79–80
Global warning system, 65–68

Goddard Space Flight Center, 7, 63, 70

GOES satellite, 17

Great Aurora (1859), 54–55

Green, James, 45–46

Greenland, 56, 80

H

Halloween storm (2003), 33, 75–76

Hamachi-LaCommare, Kristina, 61

Handwerk, Brian, 78–82

Hapgood, Mike, 49–50, 67–68

Heliophysics, Inc., 79

Highfrequency (HF) radio communications, 11, 13

Holland, Mike, 77

Hurricane Katrina, 37, 48, 52

Hydro-Quebec power grid, 11

I

Ice-core data, 56

Icelandic ash mess, 41

Intergovernmental Panel on Climate Change, 79

International Committee on Radiological Protection, 75

International Space Environment Service, 67

Interplanetary magnetic field (IMF), 25–26, 45

Ionized gas, 55, 58

Ionosphere
  defined, 24
  density disturbances, 11, 18, 24, 62
  energy deposition in, 58
  X-ray bursts in, 27–28

J

January 22, 2012 solar flare, 7–8

Japan, 44, 60

K

Kappenman, John, 46, 47, 49, 51–52, 61–62

Katrina (hurricane), 37, 48, 52

Killer flares, 27–28

Kintner, Paul, 48, 51, 52

L

Langley Research Center, 74, 76

Lawrence Berkeley National Laboratory, 61

Little Ice Age, 28

Lovett, Richard, 30–34

Low-frequency/high-consequence (LF/HC) events, 15, 71

Low Frequency (VLF) radio, 25

Lubchenco, Jane, 8–9

Lynch, Patrick, 74–77

M

M9-class flare, 8

Magnetic reconnection, 23, 26, 67

Magnetometers, 17, 45

Magnetosphere, 7, 26, 57, 58, 76

Maunder minimum, 28

Max Planck Institute for Astrophysics, 79

Max Planck Institute for Solar System Research, 81–82

Maya 2012 apocalypse, 22, 40

McCracken, Kenneth G., 56

Mertens, Chris, 76–77

Metatech Corporation, 16, 46, 61

Mount Wilson Observatory, 80

N

National Academy of Sciences, 37, 40, 44, 48–49

National Aeronautics and Space Administration (NASA)

doomsday fears and, 39, 44

Goddard Space Flight Center, 7, 63, 70

Heliospheric Division, 40

killer flares and, 28

Langley Research Center, 74

solar shield by, 69–73

space-weather predictions by, 64

space weather role of, 17–18

National Oceanic and Atmospheric Administration (NOAA)

current solar cycle impact, 35–38

space weather impact, 8

space weather predictions by, 14, 17, 60, 64

National Research Council, 10–20, 12, 33, 71

National Science Foundation, 64

Natural gas pipelines, 48

Nature (magazine), 79

Near-Earth space environment, 11

Nitrate gases, 56, 59

Non-space-weather-related events, 19

Northern/southern lights, 7, 31

Nuclear power stations, 38, 48, 77

O

Odenwald, Sten F., 53–64

O'Neill, Ian, 21–29

P

II Pegasi flare, 28

POES satellite, 17

Polar cap absorption (PCA) events, 11

Power grids

as antennas, 46

black-outs, 11, 14–16, 39

fortification of, 9

knocking out, 11, 15, 29, 62–63

outages, 12

solar flares and, 33

transformer damage, 16, 33, 46–47

Pulkkinen, Antti, 70, 72–73

R

Radiation exposure

during air travel, 7, 75–77

magnetosphere protection against, 7

from radiation storms, 32, 58

from Van Allen belt, 26, 58

Radiation-hardened electronics, 9, 19

Redd, Nola, 69–73

Reynolds, Dan, 65–68

Royal Observatory, 80

S

Satellites

aerobraking effect on, 26–27

Anik satellites, 19, 59

bracing infrastructure, 53–64
geometric storms and, 59–61
geosynchronous communications satellites, 60
GOES satellite, 17
outages, 13
in peril, 26–27
POES satellite, 17
radiation shielding for, 9
Telstar 401 satellite, 59
See also Global Positioning System (GPS) satellites
Scientific American (magazine), 55
Solanki, Sami, 81–82
Solar and Heliospheric Observatory (SOHO), 25, 51, 71
Solar Cycle 24, 8–9, 28, 35–38
Solar Dynamics Observatory, 34
Solar Electro-Optical Network, 17
Solar flares
    C-class flares, 8
    defined, 22
    January 22, 2012 solar flare, 7–8
    killer flares, 28
    M9-class flare, 8
    II Pegasi flare, 28
    power grids and, 33
    problems with, 24–25
    Valentine's Day flare, 30–31
    X-class flares, 8, 18
    X-ray flares, 24–28, 57–58
Solar shield
    against CMEs, 70–71
    under development, 72–73
    overview, 70
    for predicting solar storms, 69–73
    risk minimization with, 71–72
Solar storms
    ACE probe failure, 50–51
    danger to air travel, 74–77
    global impact of, 43–44

global warming from, 78–82
global warning system for, 65–68
Halloween storm, 33, 75–76
indifference to, 51–52
lives in jeopardy, 48–49
solutions, 52
sun's mechanics, 44–45
time for, 47–48
vulnerability to, 49–50
warning system reliability, 50
See also Coronal mass ejection (CME); Geomagnetic storms/disturbances
Solar storms, fears
    alignment matters, 25–26
    cyber cocoon rupture, 32–33
    damage from, 30–34
    doomsday fears, 22, 39–42, 44
    ground effects, 27
    killer flares, 27–28
    overview, 21–22
    predictions unreliable, 28–29
    satellite safety, 26–27
    sun cycles, 23–24
    superstorms, 53–64
    X-ray flare problems, 24–25, 26
Solar storms, socioeconomic havoc
    globally, 10–20
    industry adaptation to, 13–14
    learning from, 11–12
    overview, 11
    report on, 19–20
    vulnerabilities from, 16
Solar superstorms
    energetic protons, 58–59
    first blast, 57
    massive electric currents, 59
    overview, 54–55
    power grid outages during, 61–62
    preconditions for, 56–57

satellite infrastructure and, 53–64
second blast, 58
vulnerability to, 63–64
Solar TErrestrial RElations Observatory (STEREO), 25
Solar ultraviolet (UV) rays, 81
Solar wind, 18–19, 22, 25, 81
Space Studies Board, 71
Space weather
    forecasting, 18–19, 29, 34, 64
    impact of, 8, 12–14
    infrastructure, 17–18
    low-frequency/highconsequence (LF/HC) events, 15
    NASA role with, 17–18
    predictions, 14, 17, 60, 64
    sunspots, 23, 36, 54–57, 78–80
    terrestrial storms, 55
    See also Geomagnetic storms/disturbances; Solar flares; Solar storms
Space Weather Prediction Center (SWPC)
    forecasting capabilities, 14, 17, 18, 32, 60
    sun's activity cycle, 31, 36–38
Space.com (website), 7
Spacecraft concerns, 11–13
Spruit, Henk, 79–80
St. Cyr, Orville Chris, 63
Sudden Ionospheric Disturbances (or SIDs), 24
Sunspots, 23, 36, 54–57, 78–80
Sweden, 33, 49
Swift observatory, 28

T

Telecommunications concerns, 8, 13

Telegraph (newspaper), 40–41
Telstar 401 satellite, 59
Terrestrial storms, 55
Thomas, Brian C., 58
Transformer damage, 16, 33, 46–47

U

United Airlines, 13, 62
University of Colorado, 32, 44
University of Maryland, 56
US Air Force (USAF), 17
US Department of Defense, 17, 63
USAF Research Laboratory, 32, 33
USAF Weather Agency (AFWA), 17

V

Valentine's Day flare (2011), 30–31
Van Allen belt, 26, 58
Viereck, Rodney, 34

W

Washburn University, 58
Wide Area Augmentation System (WAAS), 13, 62

X

X-class flares, 8, 18
X-ray flares, 24–25, 26, 57–58

Z

Zheng, Yihua, 7